HOLLYWOOD SHUTDO

HOLLYWOOD SHUTDOWN

Production, Distribution, and

Exhibition in the Time of COVID

KATE FORTMUELLER

UNIVERSITY OF TEXAS PRESS ⤳ *Austin*

Requests for permission to reproduce material from this work should be
sent to:
    Permissions
    University of Texas Press
    P.O. Box 7819
    Austin, TX 78713-7819
    utpress.utexas.edu/rp-form

♾ The paper used in this book meets the minimum requirements of
ANSI/NISO Z39.48-1992 (R1997) (Permanence of Paper).

Library of Congress Control Number: 2021938613

doi:10.7560/324608

CONTENTS

ABBREVIATIONS

AMPTP   Association of Motion Picture and Television Producers
GTC   Georgia Theater Company
IATSE   International Alliance of Theatrical Stage Employees
NATO   National Association of Theater Owners
PPE   Personal protective equipment
PVOD   Premium video on demand
SAG-AFTRA   Screen Actors Guild-American Federation of Television and Radio Artists
SPE   Sony Pictures Entertainment
SXSW   South by Southwest
VOD   Video on demand
WGA   Writers Guild of America

HOLLYWOOD SHUTDOWN

HOLLYWOOD RESPONDS TO A PANDEMIC

IN 2020 HOLLYWOOD began living through its own version of Steven Soderbergh's *Contagion*. With its ensemble cast of global actors, *Contagion* resembles a 1970s disaster film, although a fictional viral pandemic subs for fires, earthquakes, or other natural disasters. Many of the elements of the film, from the Chinese origin of the virus to fervor around fake cures like forsythia (which we saw with hydroxychloroquine), seemed to materialize in our day-to-day lives, but, in most ways, the COVID-19 pandemic unfolded in an even more dramatic and chaotic fashion than Hollywood was capable of imagining.

The shutdown of physical production and the institution of work-from-home orders across the industry demonstrated a rare instance of uniform action in the business. The term "Hollywood" is often inaccurately used to paint the entertainment industry as a monolith, when in reality the industry encompasses a motley assemblage of US and global companies of various scales, film studios, television networks, streaming services, union and nonunion workers, and the many ancillary businesses and live events that support the business of "the Biz." In March 2020, when the scale of the pandemic appeared dire to many industry leaders, other producers, theater owners, and media companies defiantly announced they would continue working—only to shut down hours later. Changes happened quickly, allowing little time for industry workers or journalists to process the potential long-term ramifications of the shutdowns and stoppages before the next surprising headline appeared. CEOs and presidents would eventually be able to rely on income generated by their diversified companies, but many of the communities, workers, and regional economies that exist to support live events were left to seek out governmental support that was often slow or insufficient. Closures happened worldwide, but the financial repercussions were experienced unevenly.

Media production went on an unplanned hiatus, theme parks closed, and all forms of live events—including film festivals, concerts, theatrical film showings, live theater, and sporting events—were cancelled or paused indefinitely. As the initial shock of the pandemic began to recede, media conglomerates began to focus on strengthening their newly launched and pandemic-proof streaming services. Conglomerates like Disney and WarnerMedia had planned to integrate their streaming platforms into existing business practices in 2020, but the pandemic sped up this transition and put streaming at the center of their businesses. This is not the first time conglomerates have shifted their interdependence. In 2010 Jennifer Holt argued that the late 1980s conglomerates became increasingly dependent on television (rather than film) revenue, noting that "film and television industries have (re)negotiated their co-existence and financial interdependence, and in turn the two industries have redefined their relative importance to an entertainment conglomerate's profile."[1] In 2020 we were living through a similar moment of accelerated transformation as film and television industries redefine their position in relation to content streaming. The primary difference between the late 1980s and the beginning of the 2020s is that the COVID-19 pandemic forced conglomerates to assimilate streaming more quickly than they expected in order to maintain profit levels and stability.

Media work has always been defined by its sporadic and uncertain nature. Some of the precarity can be attributed to the competition for positions, but irregularity is an innate part of production: films are effectively short-term projects, and television productions have planned hiatuses built into production schedules. To deal with long gaps between paychecks, many television workers, such as editors and writers, can file for unemployment benefits between seasons, while actors without alternative media work can find additional jobs in service sectors such as retail or food. Understanding the total impact of the pandemic on media workers requires considering the pandemic's toll on the service sector, and in this sense acknowledging the precarity of work in Hollywood.[2] In 2020, when businesses shut down nationwide, "media and entertainment" and "service and leisure" were the hardest-hit sectors of the US economy. According to the US jobs report, in April 2020, 7.7 million people lost jobs in "leisure and hospitality," a sector that encompasses arts and entertainment as well as food services and hotel workers.[3] Much like the small businesses around the United States, many media workers relied on the CARES Act for assistance during this unexpected shutdown during pilot season—a time of year that is typically one of the busiest.

The impact of the pandemic has been immense in the media industries, but that impact can be best characterized as accelerating changes and transitions that were already in progress. As legal scholar Neil Walker suggests in his discussion of US political institutions, the pandemic has highlighted how deeply things are interconnected.[4] Hollywood businesses have always been interconnected: production stoppages impact distribution and exhibition strategy, distribution strategies influence production budgets, and movie theater closures alter global distribution strategies. The pandemic did not *highlight* new information about how sectors of the media industries are interconnected, but it did validate the benefits of conglomeration and it further entrenched power that was already deeply consolidated.

Beginning in the 1970s, US economic policies consistently favored deregulation of media industries, creating conditions favorable to conglomeration by loosening ownership caps and easing mergers and acquisitions restrictions; these changes in turn led to horizontally and vertically integrated media companies.[5] The 2018 acquisition of Time Warner by telecommunications company AT&T (which had also bought DirectTV in 2015) was not an unexpected merger of giants but the culmination of almost fifty years of policy work. For AT&T, this acquisition and the subsequent launch of the HBOMax platform would ideally drive consumers to their streaming service AT&T TV (from which audiences can access live TV and streaming apps like HBOMax) and allow the company to compete with Comcast (which controls NBCUniversal).[6] In 2019, less than a year after the close of the AT&T–Time Warner deal, Disney acquired 20th Century Fox and with it access to an extensive library of film and television content and a majority ownership of Hulu. Both of these industry-shifting mergers set the conditions for AT&T and Disney to take advantage of existing models of digital distribution, capitalize on new home exhibition practices, and, when the pandemic hit, to do so during a time when people around the world were spending months sheltering in place and avoiding large crowds.

Streaming services have been an essential part of the pandemic entertainment landscape across the United States, even as people in different states experienced other aspects of the pandemic, from the reopenings of businesses and movie theaters to regional mask ordinances, in dramatically different ways. Living in Georgia, where pandemic guidelines were loose and mask requirements controversial, I chose to limit my outings and to only patronize businesses with strict safety measures. However, since there were no restrictions on small, outdoor, socially distanced gatherings, I began to venture out to the yards of a few friends and family in May. In contrast, friends and family on the West Coast, in Washington State and California, experienced longer and more significant periods of lockdown in which even outdoor gatherings were prohibited. Despite the stricter rules in place on the West Coast, many businesses remained open and the virus continued to spread.

Hollywood Shutdown addresses how the COVID-19 pandemic altered all aspects of how Hollywood film and television is made, distributed, and watched during the pandemic. It begins with closures in China in January 2020 and moves through September 2020 in order to examine industry practices during the most expansive lockdowns and shelter-in-place orders. Writing in the immediate aftermath of historical events presents inherent challenges, and the nature of this pandemic—a prolonged period marked by multiple crisis points—presents its own particular obstacles for periodization. In addition, as of this writing, vaccination and relief plans are in place, but there is not yet an "aftermath," just a series of new challenges that further complicate the ongoing global health crisis.

In this book I define an important period—the moment of reaction and the immediate responses to the crisis—for closer examination. From January through September 2020 people around the world experienced widespread shutdowns that forced quick evaluations of existing practices. The industry instituted many significant changes to corporate structures, implemented new distribution strategies, and returned to production with new safety measures in place, but these nine months represent an initial gestation period of plans and problem solving. Decisions made in the spring and summer were positioned as temporary fixes. In order to maintain profits, some distributors seemed to be experimenting with premium video-on-demand (PVOD) releases of new films and testing the viability of theatrical releases; networks filled programming hours by reviving the Sunday Night Movie; and sports leagues eliminated fans (and stadium revenue) in order to deliver on media contracts. By September, when the United States had yet another peak in cases and epidemiologists continued to warn of a holiday surge, it was clear that studios, producers, and networks still needed a long-term plan that would project strength and stability in earnings calls and demonstrate a clear strategy for a more profitable 2021.

Many of the pandemic pivots were in fact preestablished twenty-first-century distribution and exhibition practices. When the pandemic forced Hollywood employees to work from home while people around the world sheltered in place, conglomerates and tech companies, which had been stockpiling original content and acquiring huge libraries of additional content for existing or soon-to-be-launched streaming platforms, were arguably more well positioned than they had ever been to capitalize on this situation. The most serious challenges that studios and networks faced were tied to legacy practices such as the network television cycle and theatrical windowing (guaranteeing exhibitors a certain number of weeks or months before a film moves to other distribution arms), practices that had been undergoing increased interrogation prior to the pandemic. Hollywood often embraces and celebrates new technologies, but changes to Hollywood practices and protocols tend to be incremental. In 2020, when the pandemic threatened Hollywood profits, industry leaders found themselves making quick decisions that transformed established practices in production, distribution, and exhibition in order to continue to meet consumer demands for a steady stream of new and entertaining content.

This book was written during the pandemic, which means I did not have the kind of temporal and emotional distance from my subject that is usually part of the writing process. Pandemic life and its patterns were never far from my mind: I wrote while sheltering in place, in between teaching classes on Zoom, setting up Zoom happy hours and movie nights with friends, and checking daily case numbers; all while my smiling cardboard cutout sat in Dodger Stadium for their World Series season. Although my pandemic life has been busy, it often feels a bit static, but my writing process has been complicated by the fact that the business of media also seemed to be rapidly transitioning to accommodate our pandemic viewing habits. As the months marched on, I added Starz, Shudder, and PBS Masterpiece to my streaming channels. Just to list a few of the things that happened in the media industries as I was writing this book: AT&T pushed through a major reorganization of WarnerMedia, Disney restructured to put Disney+ in charge of distribution plans for the entire company, WarnerMedia announced that it was sending its entire 2021 theatrical slate to HBOMax, larger streamers like Peacock began to assimilate some of the smaller apps, and Paramount announced the launch of its own service that subsumed the CBS All Access service. These developments do not contradict my larger argument that the pandemic is accelerating industry shifts that were already in process; rather, they underscore the fact that this book is just a starting point for wider scholarly and popular conversations about the changing contours of media conglomerates and their influence on what and how we watch film and television.

When the pandemic subsides and we are finally able to look back and consider the chain of events, we will undoubtedly notice how some small changes that seemed inconsequential resulted in monumental shifts. The social and cultural repercussions of our newfound work-from-home abilities and our makeshift pandemic solutions for online socializing will continue to shape interactions even when we return to normal, in-person socializing. Hollywood's decisions will have real and long-term influence beyond COVID-19 exigencies. *Hollywood Shutdown* uses the media industry's COVID-19 response to illustrate how the pandemic accelerated ongoing twenty-first-century trends in production, distribution, and exhibition and underscored the uneasy relationship between legacy and digital media. The changes the industry implemented—some temporary, others paradigm-shifting—will continue to reverberate in the film, television, and media industries in the decades to come.

CHAPTER I

PRODUCTION

CONTEMPORARY FILM AND TELEVISION production is a global enterprise, and, by definition, a pandemic is a global problem. Since major film and television productions are interactive and dynamic gatherings of people, all are potential superspreader events. National and regional bans on large gatherings resulted in worldwide production shutdowns and sent many offshore Hollywood casts and crews back to the United States. These stoppages obviously disrupted production schedules and delayed release dates, but they also impacted the national and regional economies that court foreign (especially US) productions.

The pandemic affected film and television production around the world to varying degrees. Specific impacts largely depended on the duration of the closure and the particular reopening procedures implemented by national, regional, and industrial leadership. As the host town of a union-dominated industry, in Hollywood this process also involved sustained negotiations between unions and producers. In the United States restarting union productions was a gradual process involving several distinct phases: complete shutdown; modified quarantine-friendly productions; productions that resumed outside of the country and in states like Georgia that reopened early; and, finally, large-scale reopening based on industry-mandated safety guidelines. Of course, not all US media is produced under union guidelines or is subject to union negotiations; the production of commercials and other nonunion projects barely stopped during the pandemic.

In the first nine months of 2020, studios, networks, production companies, and the thousands of workers who make film and television programs were tasked with adjusting their time-honored labor practices. In the United States pandemic troubleshooting also generated some distinct changes to the appearance of some of our media, especially during the spring, when creatives problem-solved a larger number of constraints. They were forced to grapple with a difficult question: How do you make media during shelter-in-place orders, statewide bans on large gatherings, and while unable to travel for location shooting? What audiences saw on screen was the result of new obstacles that posed challenges to fundamental aspects of film and television production as a group endeavor. Crews were reduced in size, onscreen talent shouldered additional tasks and risks, and producers discovered new benefits to location shooting—all before studios, networks, and unions announced approved plans for restarting production that reimagined aspects of on-set culture.

QUIET ON THE SET

In China in late January and early February, theaters, major studios like Hengdian, and productions around the country were shutting down rapidly, a foreboding of what other media industries could soon expect from the rapidly spreading coronavirus. Following these lockdowns, many foreign industry workers in China departed for their home countries in an attempt to beat border closures. Despite these disruptions, by early March (before WHO identified the spread of COVID-19 as a pandemic), some productions in China had resumed safely. As filmmaking ramped up again in China, it did so without the foreign representatives and workers who had returned to the United States and elsewhere around the world. The composition of the workforce changed. While Chinese studios were the first to close, strict shutdown measures also meant that Chinese productions (such as internationally renowned director Zhang Yimou's thriller *Impasse*, which resumed production on March 26 after a fifty-day pause) were back to work before others around the world.[1] Prior to 2020, a seven-week widespread production shutdown seemed unimaginable; after all, in 1918 the deadly Spanish flu only paused US productions for five weeks. Despite what appeared to be a strict—and long—period of industrial (and of course social) lockdown that included contact tracing and restricted access to grocery stores, assuming the case number data was accurate, China offered an example of measures that could effectively curb the spread of the virus. However, perhaps most importantly, China's battle with the virus suggested a possible timeline to reopening the economy.

As China struggled with the spread of the coronavirus, the public-facing speculation in the United States was detached. Characterizations of the virus's effect seemed primarily focused on the global financial impact of closures in the world's second-largest economy; few seemed to speculate that the coronavirus would turn into a pandemic. On February 28 one of the many *Variety* stories about China and the coronavirus announced, "Hollywood Studios Assembling Strategy Teams." Like much of the trade reporting in January and February, the article's central concern was COVID-19's impact on global distribution and exhibition; the piece offered no indication that similar disruptions could happen on American soil. The effect of theater closures around the world and the disruption of tentpole releases outside of the United States was expected to lead to billions of dollars lost in global box-office revenue. If studio teams were particularly concerned about the virus's spread in the United States, it is not apparent from the emphasis of industry reporting on COVID-19. Even in the discussions about the upcoming CinemaCon, the annual exhibitor trade show held in Las Vegas at the end of March, the focus was on the announcement that Chinese exhibitors would be absent from the event.[2] Yet only five hours after *Variety* published an article focused on the pandemic's effects on distribution and exhibition, CBS announced it would suspend production of its globetrotting reality show *The Amazing Race*. Productions such as *Mission: Impossible 7* had already shut down in response to Italy's February ban on large gatherings, but *The Amazing Race* was the first example of a proactive pause in shooting. Given the emphasis on the virus as a threat to global commerce rather than US business, it is fitting that this show was the first to take an unplanned hiatus. In hindsight, this production pause was a harbinger of things to come for US media production. Despite these early warning signs regarding film and television production, industry reporting on the virus consistently maintained that its greatest financial threat was to US film distribution; reporting often compared the COVID-19 threat to SARS, an epidemic that had been contained in Asia during 2002–2004.[3]

Hollywood films and television shows continued to shoot undeterred all over the world, from Canada to the Czech Republic. In the United States, meanwhile, television networks were in the middle of pilot season, with fifty-five pilots in production to vie for spots in the fall network lineups. However, by March 2020 US studios, networks, producers, cast, and crew responded to the pandemic's spread, mirroring China's actions by quickly shutting down domestic physical production operations and instructing employees to work from home. The nature of the pandemic made these stoppages sudden, but not unprecedented. In fact, less than six months earlier studios had been preparing for a different kind of production shutdown, one due to a strike rather than a pandemic, a situation that studios and networks have historically navigated.[4] In the late 1980s and early 1990s, and later during the 2007–2008 Writers Guild of America (WGA) strikes, television networks responded to the loss of content during union-led work stoppages by developing and producing reality television.[5] The development of reality television demonstrates how innovations—such as relying on hosts to minimize cast size and star salaries and compiling real-life events into a narrative or compilation shows—can emerge out of the need to develop new programming even when the media industries are ostensibly shut down. As was the case with reality television, short-term strategies to get around union workers can have a long-term effect on production and programming strategies.[6] Producers have grown accustomed to stoppages and have learned how to prepare for them, yet the pandemic still unsettled the rhythms of productions in unprecedented ways as well as disrupting many of the service and leisure industries that provide necessary income to freelance creatives. It would require creativity, careful planning, and financial resources to get film and television production back on track.

Although the coronavirus had been spreading worldwide since December 2019, the appearance of the virus in the United States and the dawning realization that the viral epidemic in China had become a full-fledged pandemic seemed to have a sudden and dramatic effect on Hollywood film and television productions. Beginning on March 10, 2020, shutdown announcements appeared in rapid succession. Those reading *Deadline*, *Variety*, and the *Hollywood Reporter* in real-time likely experienced whiplash trying to keep up with delays and closures. Networks and producers would announce their intent to continue production only to change course a day later. Plans for delayed film releases became dizzying as studios evaluated release strategies and dates on a case-by-case basis. Nobody had a clear idea of how long the industry would need to stay shut down. Amid these initial shut-down notices, A-list stars Tom Hanks and Rita Wilson announced that they had both tested positive during the production of Baz Luhrman's Elvis movie in Australia and were resting and recovering in isolation in that country. Hanks, a beloved figure, became one of the first stars to test positive (or at least to publicly admit to testing positive), adding to the sense of an escalating crisis in a way that sheer numbers could not capture. In a matter of a few weeks, the coronavirus had gone from a concern in a few isolated hot spots to a matter of global interest affecting every major US motion picture and television production around the world and infecting a well-known and loved US star.

In the United States live broadcasts and talk shows, many with studio audiences of hundreds of people, comprise a significant part of daily television programming. Producers of these shows found themselves scrambling to manage the pandemic, as no network wanted the spread of the virus connected to one of their productions. Networks announced on March 12 that talk shows including *The Ellen DeGeneres Show*, *Jimmy Kimmel Live*, *The Late Show with Stephen Colbert*, and *The Daily Show with Trevor Noah* would continue production without live studio audiences—only to turn around one day later and completely suspend production. Shows that remained on the air, such as *CBS This Morning*, saw crews and employees moving from their regular, centralized location to many different locations, including the Ed Sullivan Theater, in order to accommodate deep cleaning and distancing.

Since many of these programs serve as the primary news source for Americans, the idea of a total media production shutdown was never a possibility. Pauses in scripted productions have a significant impact on budgets and long-term effects on release calendars, which was enough financial incentive for many productions to attempt to continue shooting. However, when authorities in Los Angeles and New York announced shelter-in-place orders on March 19 and 20, respectively, many of the last holdouts were forced to shut down. National travel bans and broader closures sent cast and crew members working outside the country scrambling to get back into the United States. Over the course of the last two weeks of March, the trades consistently reported a cascade of production shutdowns, despite the best efforts of producers to continue working with enhanced sanitation procedures.

The effect of these shutdowns was experienced in myriad ways as studio heads and CEOs, network presidents, showrunners, and producers considered how to balance the complex web of production schedules. The long-running CW series *Supernatural* paused production before shooting its series finale, and producers were left to speculate as to how and when they would be able to resume production and how their new schedule would work with star Jared Padalecki's role in the forthcoming CW reboot of *Walker, Texas Ranger*. In contrast, daytime soap operas, which shoot many weeks ahead of airing, had approximately four to six weeks of new episodes ready to broadcast when they paused production.[7] Other shows and films simply had to delay the start of production indefinitely. Although some shows, such as streaming successes *Lucifer* and the critically acclaimed *The Handmaid's Tale*, were able to resume production in September, other producers and cast members found out that their shows—including *GLOW*, *The Society*, *Stumptown*, and *I'm Sorry*—would be cancelled later in the summer and early fall, moves that were publicly attributed to pandemic-related budget cuts.

Budgetary concerns also stemmed from unresolved questions about financial liability raised by unanticipated production suspensions. Amid the pandemic closures, one of the primary questions producers asked was: Who is responsible for payments to those individuals with contractual guarantees—the studios or the insurance companies? The full scope of financial losses as well as the future of insurance policies was still unclear during the spring and summer.

However, industry leaders, lawyers, and producers all seemed, at least initially, to agree that COVID-19 delays would not be covered on new policies whenever the industry reopened. Although issues of production insurance remained in flux in the spring of 2020, big-budget studio films resumed, although securing insurance would emerge as a crucial challenge for independent films seeking to revive production.[8]

In the immediate aftermath of production stoppages in March, actors, grips, makeup artists, cinematographers, and others all found themselves out of work, but closures did not affect all entertainment workers equally. While some, such as A-list actors, had salary guarantees in their contracts, many below-the-line workers did not, a group that includes crew members from costumers to grips, who work for predetermined hourly wages rather than a negotiated salary. The unions and guilds who support these workers found themselves scrambling to assist suddenly out-of-work creatives. Because media work is sporadic, unions and guilds know that many of their members may require support during lean employment periods and offer programs to subsidize them during emergencies. The pandemic, however, created an overwhelming demand for these services. In the wake of shutdowns, the unions and guilds issued statements in which they advocated for federal support and strategized different plans to financially assist members during the closures.

Members of the International Alliance of Theatrical Stage Employees (IATSE), which consists of numerous craft and technical locals, were particularly concerned with the loss of jobs. In the wake of a positive test on the Chicago set of *NeXt*, Local 600 (the International Cinematographers Guild) expressed fears that its members might not be hired if producers began acting more cautiously than required by federal and state guidelines. When shutdowns became more widespread, IATSE scrambled to support members. By May 2020 the media industry had lost 120,000 jobs—part of ballooning unemployment numbers nationwide; reportedly 890,000 people were out of work in the Los Angeles–area film and television industries alone.[9]

Across the trades, the screen performers' union, SAG-AFTRA, emerged as one of the most cautious unions early in the pandemic.

In its March 13 announcement, SAG-AFTRA warned members not to travel to or report for work in China, Italy, Iran, or South Korea. Actors know that the very nature of their work puts them at greater risk than others on set. In March scientists were still unclear about many aspects of COVID-19, including whether the virus spread through surface contact and/or aerosols, but epidemiologists were advising people to avoid crowds, wash their hands frequently, and not touch their faces. For members of SAG-AFTRA, working in crowds, touching their faces, and engaging in regular close contact with other actors, makeup artists, and hairstylists constitute a normal day on set. Avoiding these common behaviors would render the world of the film unnatural. The union's concern about actors putting themselves at risk for their craft contributed to the consistent safety warnings and "Do not work" reminders.[10]

The pandemic also highlighted one of the preexisting problems in the entertainment industry: many of its workers cobble together a living through multiple gigs. In Hollywood, as elsewhere, many workers are freelance, which means that they are accustomed to periods of unemployment. Workers rely on the busy periods for financial support during the lean times. If they are unable to fully support themselves though media work, they make a living through a variety of jobs or side hustles. The sweeping closures of businesses where people gather (especially bars, restaurants, gyms, and concert venues) meant that not only did production work disappear, so did other part-time work. For example, in an interview for *The Business* podcast, actor David Saucedo explained that at the start of the pandemic, few people were interested in touching old records and vintage clothes (his business alongside acting work).[11] The ubiquity of stories like Saucedo's showcases the reality that many media workers are unable to make a living through media work alone and can be thrown into a precarious existence during any economic or health crisis.

For many who make their living in Hollywood, instability is a characteristic of their work; storied support funds provide some assistance, including the Actors Fund (established in 1882), the Authors League Fund (established in 1917), and the Motion Picture and Television Fund (established in 1921). In addition, specific union foundations have long assisted Hollywood workers in crises. The spring and summer of 2020 also saw a number of temporary assistance programs set up by large companies such as Netflix and individuals such as Liz Alper, cofounder of #PayUpHollywood, which advocates for higher assistant pay. That organization jumped in to raise money for out-of-work personal assistants through GoFundMe. Yet these internal support structures were insufficient to the scale of this crisis, and all of the unions were vocal about the importance of federal support for media and entertainment workers who found themselves out of work from the middle of March onward. Through website announcements and statements in the trades, unions encouraged members to contact congressional representatives and advocate for an aid package that would support freelance workers in the media industries who often do not fit conventional unemployment definitions.

As a global industry, Hollywood's entertainment conglomerates negotiated the spread of the coronavirus since January 2020. Although slow to acknowledge the pandemic and prepare for stoppages, Hollywood ultimately reacted swiftly once the virus began to spread around the country and infect cast and crew. The year 2020 might be remembered (at least in part) as the year in which Hollywood ground to a halt, but in reality, the large-scale films and scripted shows that shut down were mainly the high-profile productions of major networks and studios. Although some unplanned hiatuses might have offered networks an opportunity to cancel underperforming or expensive shows, most of these shutdowns were temporary. Much work was still happening in media—ideas continued to be pitched, deals were continually made, and unions continued with their contract negotiations. Further, although actors, cinematographers, directors, makeup artists, and many others had ceased working on set, those who worked in postproduction and animation were able to continue virtually throughout the shelter-in-place orders. In addition, nonunion films, commercials, and talk shows pivoted quickly and improvised to continue meeting audience demand. The shutdown was monumental, but the media produced during quarantine can tell us more about how the pandemic will continue to transform Hollywood practices into the near future.

MEDIA PRODUCTION DURING QUARANTINE

While lockdowns in theory gave Americans the time to consume media as never before, much of the springtime content that they were used to enjoying was just not available. In the United States spring brings college basketball's March Madness, the NHL playoffs, the NBA playoffs, and the start of the MLB season. Television networks rely on these sporting events to generate significant advertising revenue (not to mention millions for Las Vegas sports books), but the swift cancellation of March Madness, delays in both NHL and NBA postseason play, and a postponement and shortening of the MLB season hurt the bottom line for broadcast networks, cable channels, and casinos (which had to refund cancelled bets), and left fans around the country without sports during the peak period of national lockdown. For television audiences and producers alike, the lack of live sports content created a problem.

Spring also marks the beginning of the season of big-budget and high-revenue films that anchor annual income reports for studios, the so-called tentpole movies. In 2020 the tentpole releases should have begun with *Mulan* on March 27. With major franchise installments, including *No Time to Die* (the twenty-fifth Bond film), *F9* (the ninth *Fast and Furious* installment), and *Minions 2: The Rise of Gru* delayed to 2021, studios sent a message, at least initially, that they would be withholding premium content for an eventual reopening of theater venues. Audiences met this dramatic lack of theatrical film releases (and network television's spring programming landscape) by searching for alternatives. Announcements of production shutdowns and cast and crew quarantines poured into *Deadline, Variety,* and the *Hollywood Reporter,* along with speculation about how this might impact the future of the theatrical release schedule and the fall pilot season. By March 16, fifty-eight scripted shows had announced shutdowns or postponements, and by late March thirty-five film productions had announced delays. Production shutdowns were shocking and disruptive, but media production never stopped. Finales, soap operas, daily and weekly live shows, a few quarantine productions, and select Netflix productions that were shooting in nations that had been more successful at containing the virus were all made—with minor pauses and hiccups—throughout the height of the COVID-19 case spikes in the spring.

Perhaps the most notable exceptions to the pandemic shutdowns were computer-based media productions: animated projects, post-production work, and digital effects workshops all continued with minimal interruption, in contrast to live-action productions. In the case of postproduction work, editors operating off hard drives were able to finish up their existing projects from home. Of course, many editors expressed concern after the first week of shutdown that without new footage they would likely be out of work.[12] However, animated shows continued to be created largely unfettered throughout the spring.[13] Although animators have to deal with the challenges of uploading enormous files using home internet connections, animation studios already have fairly established workflows that allow actors to provide self-taped auditions and record their voice work off-site. Voice actors have lamented many of the changes to auditions that require them to self-direct and record their work, but in the pandemic climate these established remote practices could largely continue as usual.[14] Companies such as Bento Box (which is responsible for *Bob's Burgers*) were doing so well that they were able to hire additional freelancers in March, when many companies were laying off workers.[15]

Studios lamented the spring and summer shutdown and the loss of the tentpole revenue, and production companies and networks in the process of making shows to air for the fall season saw the arrival of the pandemic in the middle of March as possibly the worst timing for their production model. In contrast to this seasonal model, streaming platforms distinguish themselves with a steady flow of new content throughout the calendar year and are not beholden to the same network production and premiere calendar. Netflix, which has long positioned itself as a disruptor of conventional schedules and distribution, was vocal during its first quarter earnings call (which took place on April 21) in noting that the timing of the pandemic was irrelevant for its production schedule.[16] Although Netflix assured shareholders that the pandemic had no impact on its distribution schedule for 2021, the company did not offer any specifics on this point. However, Netflix subscribers and readers of industry trades could clearly see that despite its confident messaging, the streaming service shifted to pandemic-specific content and sought out alternative filming locations around the world.

The demand for films, television shows, and commercials never slowed, but the disrupted production landscape introduced tremendous variation in the ways that producers met audience demands. The majority of productions temporarily paused while the Association of Motion Picture and Television Producers (AMPTP) and film and television guilds and unions could come up with a safe way to restart filming. Along with Netflix, several networks experimented with remote production methods to create films and limited series about quarantine and the pandemic. Early on, there were three projects made about the pandemic and within production restrictions: Jenji Kohan's project, *Social Distance*, was announced in late April, but even before that show reached audiences, the Netflix short documentary series *Homemade*, HBO's *Coastal Elites*, and Freeform's *Love in the Time of Corona* all beat it to air. In order to film, producers found creative, safe workarounds, such as casting real-life couples who were already in quarantine together or providing actors with the production tools to film themselves. Films such as *Malcolm and Marie* and *Locked Down* would use similar production workarounds in the summer and fall. These early shows all attempted to reflect on the human experience of the pandemic, but despite casting recognizable actors, these pandemic-centered stories and their reliance on Zoom and claustrophobic camerawork too closely resembled our own dull, real-life pandemic experiences. The responses to these experiments in remote production were critically mixed, but their production histories and the films and television shows themselves all document the labor conditions and the experience of media-making in the pandemic.

Some shows embraced safe modes of production that clearly seemed to be temporary solutions, such as filming an episode or finale on Zoom, like *RuPaul's Drag Race*, or enlisting an animation team for a special episode like showrunner Gloria Calderón Kellett arranged for *One Day at a Time* (*ODAT*). *The Daily Show with Trevor Noah* took a different approach and reinvented aspects of the show as *The Daily Social Distancing Show with Trevor Noah* (*DSDS*) in a way that embraced rather than attempted to ignore the ongoing pandemic. These different approaches to pandemic media production ranged from no changes to temporary pivots to fundamental adjustments to the norms of production, and in doing so they function as a microcosm for the fragmented COVID plans and responses around the United States. As case studies, *ODAT* and the *DSDS* showcase inventive responses to the reality of the pandemic, and, as cable shows they also reveal some of the freedoms of working for a cable network in contrast with the narrower set of options available at the broadcast networks.

ONE DAY AT A TIME

Even prior to the pandemic, *ODAT* had a tumultuous run, airing for three seasons on Netflix before getting cancelled, only to be renewed for a fourth season on cable's Pop TV. Season 4 was in production in front of a live studio audience when the pandemic hit. On March 10, after shooting only four episodes, *ODAT* eliminated its live audience, making the show one of the first to adapt production to the rapidly growing concern around the pandemic. Although they were quick to pivot, cast and crew were only able to complete two more episodes without an audience before *ODAT* fully suspended production. With only six out of the planned thirteen episodes completed and no clear way to resume production in the foreseeable future, showrunner Gloria Calderón Kellett began considering alternative ways to continue making season 4 of the show.

Throughout the spring, Calderón Kellett seemed omnipresent in the trades because of her proactive handling of the pandemic. A few days after the production shutdowns, Calderón Kellett took to Twitter to ask: "Industry folks: Can we have a real & honest conversation about the realities that need to be in place for us to return to work safely?" These Twitter exchanges, which she initiated well before the unions officially announced their committee plans for reopening, were summarized as part of a series of articles about reopening in *Deadline*.[17] The series addressed a wide array of strategies, from the necessity of daily testing to ideas about how to create production bubbles. Many of these ideas were circulating elsewhere in the

trades, on individual companies' plans, and on social media throughout the spring. Calderón Kellett also addressed a couple points that
were specific to her show: first, her concern about the safety of an
older star, Rita Moreno, and the producer, Norman Lear, who fall
into vulnerable categories; and second, apprehension about how
much hugging and kissing is featured on the family sitcom and when
she would feel safe asking actors to be that close.

Even as Calderón Kellett considered how to return to set in early
March, she was simultaneously planning the logistics to produce an
animated episode of her show. As one of the few shows in production in April and May, "The Politics Episode" of *ODAT* was touted
consistently in the trades because of its approach to production,
its guest stars (Lin-Manuel Miranda and Gloria Estefan), and its
timely topic (how to have difficult family conversations about the
2020 election). This animated episode of *ODAT* was completed on
a shortened timeline, taking seven to eight weeks rather than seven
to eight months usually required to produce a thirty-minute animated episode.[18] Once the animation team was on board, the showrunners worked on getting sound equipment and a sound technician
to facilitate recording. Coverage in *Variety*, *Deadline*, and the *Hollywood Reporter* does not have the same audience reach as late-night
talk shows, but presence in the trades keeps a show (and in this case
the showrunner) relevant in industry conversations. Her innovative
solution for producing media in the pandemic positions *ODAT* as
a noteworthy and unusual case demonstrating the range of Hollywood's pandemic response.

"The Politics Episode" is visually different from other episodes of
ODAT and seems to embrace many of the conventions of animated
prime-time shows. Animated family sitcoms, such as *The Simpsons*,
Family Guy, *King of the Hill*, and others, have been a staple of prime-
time television since *The Simpsons* premiered in 1989. Although these
shows often resemble traditional sitcoms, as Michael Tueth argues,
the animated sitcom emerged in the 1990s to "liberate the domestic sitcom from the straightjacket of visual naturalism."[19] Whereas
ODAT is a traditional multicamera sitcom, the animated episode
stylizes emotions, embraces visual gags (such as exploding heads),
and tells its story in a nonlinear fashion. According to Mike Royce

and Calderón Kellett, the flashback structure of the episode was always part of the script, which made this episode particularly suited to animation.[20]

ODAT is yet another example of how the pandemic exacerbated existing problems in the entertainment industry that predate 2020. The show's story of cancellation and renewal speaks to the nature of contemporary television production, in which shows such as *Buffy the Vampire Slayer*, which moved from the WB to UPN, have their plotlines, seasons, and industrial histories shaped by network turmoil. In the case of *ODAT*, its path (from streaming to cable to network) and the multiple resurrections speak to the increased demands for content in the on-demand, streaming era. Since the show centers on a Cuban-American family, it would also seem that *ODAT* could be one answer to audience requests for—and network searches for—shows featuring BIPOC (Black, Indigenous, People of Color) characters and experiences. Supported by executives at Pop TV, *ODAT* found creative workarounds to produce episodes amid production shutdowns and solutions to keep the show in the public eye despite marketing disruption. Unfortunately for the producers, the show itself seemed to be more resilient than the network that supported it during the tumultuous production of season four. Although *ODAT* had a thirteen-episode order, "The Politics Episode" (episode 7) was the last episode of season 4 due to both the prolonged shutdown and organizational disruption at Pop TV. In late September *ODAT* got a third chance for renewal from CBS. Faced with huge gaps in its programming schedule as a result of production delays, CBS announced that it would air the first six episodes of *ODAT* in prime time; but against the showrunners' wishes, it would not air the animated episode the week before election night. Thus, while Sony Television Productions and Pop TV supported and aired the timely animated episode, CBS shied away from the politically charged content of the episode. From production to content, the post-Netflix afterlife of *ODAT* showcases some of the differences between network and cable programming in the twenty-first century, differences that were also brought into relief with talk-show production during the pandemic.

THE DAILY SOCIAL DISTANCING SHOW WITH TREVOR NOAH

Shooting talk shows from home requires creativity to distinguish the nightly television shows from audience members' daily Zoom meetings. After a brief attempt to produce shows without an audience, daily and nightly programs ceased production just as scripted film and television shows had in mid-March. A key feature of the talk-show format is its consistent, daily appearance in the television programming schedule. For some viewers, talk shows (such as *Today*) are part of a daily routine and serve as a morning soundtrack; others use talk shows, such as *The Daily Show with Trevor Noah*, to keep up with the news. In early spring many viewers in the United States were focused not only on the pandemic but on the 2020 primary election and the many delayed races around the country. In order to maintain their presence, and, in some cases, for hosts to sustain their relevance as cultural critics and commentators, these shows had to find a way to resume production during state shelter-in-place orders.

Talk shows had to adapt their visual styles in order to stay on the air in the spring. Amid inevitable diminishing production values, some shows leaned into gimmicks and embraced the collapse between private and workspace that characterized this widespread shift to work-from-home. Each show looked a little different: Stephen Colbert shot a video from his bathtub; Samantha Bee enlisted her family members to shoot *Beeing at Home with Samantha Bee!* in the woods of her upstate New York home; and Jimmy Fallon talked to guests via Zoom for *The Tonight Show Starring Jimmy Fallon: At Home Edition*. For many of these shows, the name and format changes were temporary, and beginning in July network hosts such as Jimmy Fallon resumed shooting in the studio even as US COVID numbers peaked beyond those of the March shutdown. While network shows returned to the studio and, like much of the country, attempted to project normalcy, cable shows had the flexibility to continue remote production. As Trevor Noah explained about his decision to continue shooting his show from home: "I do not wish to make the same mistake America made, and that is rushing to go back to normal when nothing is normal."[21]

The Daily Show with Trevor Noah, which became *The Daily Social Distancing Show with Trevor Noah* on March 18, has been one of the more successful pivots from studio to living-room production. After earning a 24-percent ratings boost in the 18–34 age group in April, Comedy Central decided to change Noah's thirty-minute comedy news show to a forty-five-minute program for the duration of the pandemic. Linear viewing did see a bump in viewership during the first two months of the pandemic in the United States, but the growth of *DSDS* was significant for a show that was initially slow to gain viewers.[22] In contrast, *DSDS* chose to continue to embrace the work-from-home aesthetic well after *Jimmy Kimmel Live*, *The Tonight Show Starring Jimmy Fallon*, and others returned to the studio. The result has been both a more intimate variation of the late-night format and a production that decisively refuses to pretend that the world is normal.

DSDS first aired on YouTube, offering much of the same content and commentary of *The Daily Show*. The existing digital team and infrastructure were an essential part of the show's continued visibility. In an interview with *Variety*, showrunner Jennifer Flanz explained that the digital team continued to put up content throughout the closure, so they already had infrastructure and a platform to release digital versions of the show. For the early episodes of *DSDS*, Noah sported what would become his trademark monochrome hooded sweatshirt and was seated on a couch in front of a refreshingly minimalist and geometrically interesting bookshelf. Broadcast networks often recommend bookshelves as a background for remote appearances because they add a bit of color and dimension to the frame, but the ubiquity of this setting has become an oft-mocked accessory of the pandemic. Commentary on backgrounds has become the subject of Twitter feeds like @BCredibility and @ratemyskype-room, and the *New York Times* quipped that bookshelves added "a patina of authority to . . . amateurish video feeds."[23] Noah's background, much like his apparel and framing, presented a slightly elevated version of typical Zoom compositions for the thousands of people who were working from their own couches around the United States. Because *The Daily Show* team understood that pandemic closures would be much longer than two weeks, they worked on getting

The first episode of *The Daily Social Distancing Show* (March 18, 2020).

episodes shot in Noah's New York apartment rather than a Comedy Central studio.

As a show on a cable network, Noah was allowed to make this decision and articulate his rationale for continuing to work from home. He has also reportedly been paying the salaries of his twenty-five furloughed crew members during the pandemic, which has likely allowed them to continue to work safely from home.[24] The format of *DSDS* clearly reflects Noah's critique that the United States reopened businesses prematurely, and his production process presents his vision of best practices during the pandemic.

Cable networks—and the talk shows that fill many of their time slots—speak to niche audiences across the spectrum of interests and politics. *DSDS* marks a historical shift in the nature of the talk-show format. As scholars and media commentators have pointed out, from the 1970s to the 1990s, network talk-show monologues were frequently considered to be a barometer of the public's "common sense" about politics and society.[25] In the case of cable hosts, monologues can be honed to speak to a smaller audience segment and reflect a clearer political position. In 2020 the production and aesthetics of late-night shows on the networks were as revealing of politics as the monologues.

The virus response in the United States has been inconsistent and divisive. Over the course of the spring and summer of 2020, decisions to reopen became clearly politicized: conservatives and right-wing politicians ignored science and public health concerns and loudly advocated to reopen the economy. Acknowledging the pandemic, wearing masks, and following the advice of scientists were labeled partisan actions. Broadcast talk-show productions mirrored the muddled US pandemic response that claimed that simply reopening businesses could effect a return to normal. In contrast, cable hosts such as Noah, who cater to a niche audience, could make value-based decisions about their shows and model practices and behaviors that he believed *should* be common sense.

Cable networks offered greater flexibility for shows like *ODAT* and *DSDS* during the pandemic. Throughout the spring and summer of 2020, the studios and shows that were most adaptable and inventive were those that aired on networks that allowed more autonomy over production and format. As in the case of *ODAT*, innovative showrunner pivots did not necessarily mean a show was immune to the network turnover and disruption that hit all aspects of the industry. However, for other shows, such as *DSDS*, a greater degree of creative freedom yielded growth. Regardless of outcome, pandemic pivots reflected a dynamic media environment even while the industry was ostensibly shutdown.

BEFORE THE REOPEN: LOCATION SHOOTING FROM Y'ALLYWOOD TO SOUTH KOREA

During the COVID-19 shutdown, locations with looser restrictions or better testing protocols offered producers the opportunity to resume shooting while most European nations and media hubs such as Los Angeles and New York remained under shelter-in-place orders. During the spring and summer, filmmakers had two options for resuming production: they could look to foreign countries that had curbed the spread of the virus, or they could consider taking advantage of the early reopening in Republican-led states such as Georgia. Producers were eager to resume production, and whether they simply wanted to avoid controversy or were legitimately concerned about worker safety, in the early months of the pandemic this meant leaving California and New York. Instead of offering financial benefits or scenic vistas, locations outside of Hollywood in 2020 offered safer working conditions, favorable government policies, and, possibly, infrastructure to support regular COVID-19 testing.

Foreign location shooting has been a staple of Hollywood productions since the years following World War II. Films, and increasingly television shows, depend on nonstudio locations to establish authenticity for their narrative worlds, and producers expect US states and foreign nations to entice them with tax incentives. Oftentimes directors will cite both reasons to justify location shooting. In his analysis of location shooting during World War II, Daniel Steinhart explains that "the distinction became debatable": Do films require overseas locations for authenticity, or is that claim merely a convenient excuse for directors seeking advantageous financial terms?[26] In the postwar period, studios took advantage of the many tax breaks implemented by European nations—economic incentives that were designed to help rebuild war-ravaged film industries and economies—and such arrangements became a staple of Hollywood productions. Similarly, in the late twentieth and early twenty-first centuries, various US states have designed tax incentives to court the film industry with the hope of developing new information economies in struggling regions. Whatever the reasons offered for justifying location shooting, the rationale for this practice has been remarkably consistent throughout the history of filmmaking. That is, until the coronavirus pandemic presented unexpected rationales for location shooting.

In trade outlets and on social media, producers such as Gloria Calderón Kellett and Tyler Perry and CEOs such as Ted Sarandos of Netflix frequently echoed the advice of epidemiology experts: increased COVID-19 testing was a prerequisite for safe reopening. However, in March and April, the United States was struggling with a shortage of testing supplies, and even when tests were available, they could not be processed quickly. In contrast, smaller nations, such as Iceland, were testing a larger percentage of their population and were able to effectively contain the spread. Restarting production in the United States amid the pandemic was not something producers could quickly troubleshoot, as it was dependent on a strong national response to the crisis. As the United States floundered, Hollywood relied on its global networks to reopen production elsewhere.

The global infrastructure of the industry was briefly considered to be a liability in the beginning of the pandemic. In January and February studios were, at least publicly, only expressing concerns about the effect of the coronavirus on international offices and productions, and Hollywood's global locations were among the first to shut down production. But by April Hollywood began to rely on its infrastructure outside of the United States as this country struggled to get the virus under control. Moving productions to foreign locations became an asset in the attempt to restart film and television production. In April director Baltasar Kormakur chose to relocate to Iceland to resume shooting his Netflix supernatural series *Kalta*. Iceland had tested 10 percent of its (much smaller) national population, so the spread of the virus was more contained. Restarting production included a variety of steps, such as creating color-coded pods (to provide quick visual indicators of where people were allowed on set) and frequent testing. Initially Kormakur avoided shooting intimate scenes out of an abundance of caution. Netflix, Kormakur noted, was also extremely supportive of the safety measures and continued to pay cast and crew who were required to quarantine (after testing positive) during shooting.[27] The strategies outlined above are similar to those adopted by the US unions.

Netflix, which had been expanding its global market by producing as well as distributing increased content outside of the United States, was particularly well-situated for these pandemic conditions. During Netflix's upbeat first quarter earnings call in April, executives touted growing subscriber numbers and highlighted the viral success of *Tiger King: Murder, Mayhem and Madness* as well as flogging its forthcoming shows, but in response to questions about production delays, CEO and Chief Content Officer Ted Sarandos confidently explained that the pandemic would not impact any of Netflix's 2021 release dates. Of course, Netflix was not immune to production shutdowns, and some of its most reportedly popular shows such as *Stranger Things* and *The Witcher* shut down production in March. Sarandos's explanation for his lack of concern was that the company operates on a more flexible production schedule than the rest of the media industry and shoots well in advance of release dates, essentially stockpiling content for binge-conducive releases throughout the year.

In spite of this claim of stockpiled content, Netflix was quick to resume productions around the world for its global content, beginning with two productions in Iceland. By July Netflix had resumed twenty-two of its productions around the world.[28] Like much of the information Netflix publicly releases, comments about production were both upbeat and opaque. Regardless of whether the streaming service was concerned about its production schedules, Netflix undoubtedly had a wider array of options for resuming production than producers based solely or primarily in the United States.

Because the United States lacked a cohesive federal plan for containing the virus and reopening businesses, the states were left to craft their own plans instead, which made for a haphazard return to film production. In Los Angeles, unions, producers, and health care professionals coordinated a plan to restart production. Elsewhere, such as in Georgia, production standards were led by the state government. When many states remained under shelter-in-place orders and businesses remained closed, in early April Georgia governor Brian Kemp pushed to reopen businesses such as bowling alleys, nail salons, and tattoo parlors by the end the month. The state guidelines for resuming film production in Georgia followed in May. The "nonbinding" guidelines issued by the state identify some general—and at times contradictory—suggestions for how to resume productions. The preventative measures recommend wearing appropriate personal protective equipment (PPE) but also stress that workers should cover their mouths with a tissue when they sneeze, advice that seems unnecessary if everyone is wearing masks. Guidelines are phrased as gentle suggestions: "If possible, reduce the number of extras in a scene."[29] Further, while many in the industry believed that frequent testing was a prerequisite for resuming production, the Georgia guidelines do not discuss testing until page six, and the testing section simply states: "Production companies may decide to require some type of testing protocol."[30] This open-ended description is out of sync with broader industry discussions, and it is phrased in such a way that it fails to constitute a guideline. Rather than taking a stance to promote the safety of Georgians and actively promote best policies, this guide served more as an announcement that film production in Georgia was open for business while much of Hollywood was not.

Georgia was open, but Hollywood did not rush to resume production in the early months of May and June. Commercials (for companies like Domino's that wanted to highlight their pandemic-friendly delivery practices) and music videos began shooting in Georgia under these guidelines, with agents vetting the safety protocols for their clients. Despite being open, film and television production in Georgia did not resume in earnest until Tyler Perry began production on his show *Sistas* in early July. Tyler Perry Studios crafted a plan to turn his studio, on a former military base, into "Camp Quarantine." While the state's regulations were lax, Perry's thirty-page studio guidelines were extensive. His plan to reopen his studio to film both *Sistas* and *The Oval* relied on creating a production bubble. This model, in which people quarantined together by working and living on-site, resembled the NBA Bubble that had been approved by June for implementation in late July. The NBA Bubble, which was housed at Walt Disney World, had a built-in quarantine with its training camp and exhibition games throughout July. Television productions, however, require a quicker schedule. In many ways Perry's setup was ideal for resuming production. Cast and crew were transported to the studio by Perry's private jet and a studio shuttle; they were rapid-tested immediately upon arrival; and they resided on site at the 330-acre Atlanta studio, which had formerly housed soldiers, for the duration of production. This included Perry, who lived in his old Madea tour bus and received regular testing throughout the shoots. Although not every production or studio could accommodate cast and crew on site, the testing procedures Perry implemented offered practices that other productions could strive to replicate.

The first tentpole production resumed in England in mid-July with *Jurassic World: Dominion*, a darkly humorous exclamation point to one of the recurring internet jokes of the summer of 2020. Throughout the spring and summer, *McSweeney's Internet Tendency* and Twitter wits joked about the fictional reopening of *Jurassic Park*: @relentlessbored tweeted, "I owe the Jurassic Park franchise an apology, it is in fact very realistic the rich would reopen a park in spite of it consistently resulting in mass death."[31] Some exceptional factors allowed *Jurassic World: Dominion* to resume filming, including the fact that Universal allowed an additional $3 million to be spent on safety protocols, such as hiring an outside medical facility to handle testing. Additionally, the film was able to resume production under its original insurance policy, which meant that the production would be covered in the event of COVID-19 shutdowns.[32] *Jurassic World* became the model for implementing COVID-19 safety procedures on big-budget productions. Although the set was largely COVID-free, the film had to pause production for two weeks in October after several positive tests.

Similar to the patchwork of state-controlled reopening plans in the United States, guidelines for resuming production varied wildly across studios and production companies. However, the Hollywood productions that recommenced over the summer—whether in Iceland, Georgia, or the United Kingdom—relied heavily on regular testing of cast and crew.

While many productions waited for national leadership and were forced to coordinate across multiple studios, Tyler Perry was in an exceptional situation. He has a history as a producer who disregards unions, and he owns his own studio in a right-to-work state that reopened quickly. Speaking about his experience restarting production, Perry reflected, "I don't know how anyone in Hollywood is going to shoot without daily testing or quarantine bubbles."[33] In order for a widespread return to film and television production, unions, producers, executives, cast, and crew all needed to develop and implement procedures that would work not just in exceptional cases but for *all* productions.

THE UNITED STATES RETURNS TO SET

In the rush to revive production, new safety plans emerged alongside the medical and scientific communities' developing understanding of the coronavirus. In the early months of the pandemic, the primary production across the United States seemed to be our collective performance of what journalists termed "hygiene theater."[34] People sanitized their mail and wore gloves to the grocery store in an attempt to stave off the virus. To help reverse the economic downturn, businesses put their minimum-wage workers and custodial staff at risk constantly cleaning and sterilizing high-touch surfaces in an attempt to make people comfortable enough to leave their homes. The capitalist logic of this—that by finding the elusive Clorox Wipes and using them vigilantly we could disinfect ourselves out of the pandemic—was like a twisted version of the neoliberal notion that anyone can pull herself up by her bootstraps. As we would come to learn, we could not disinfect our way back to normal.

The fixation on cleaning and surface transmission shaped some of the early reopening plans. Independent producers Brian Kavanaugh-Jones and Chris Ferguson proposed a strategy for smaller-budget films that relied on quarantining, reducing the number of people on set, and closing off the set for three days to allow the virus time to die on surfaces.[35] Similarly, early studio plans, such as the Lionsgate Safety Guidelines, placed sanitation as one of the four pillars (along with social distancing, enforcement, and change) of their return-to-set guidelines. In the earliest months, these plans developed despite an incomplete picture of how the virus spread. As scientific understandings improved, many of these plans adapted, but certain core principles about reducing people on set and identifying the essential personnel within groups remained part of the production plans formalized between the AMPTP and the Hollywood unions.

While productions resumed in select countries around the world, US producers and the guilds had to collaborate on a plan to get casts and crew back to set. The first of these documents was a white paper released on June 1 and coauthored by the Industry-Wide Labor-Management Safety Committee Task Force comprised of the AMPTP, all of the unions and guilds, and several health officials. The white paper was an unusual collaboration between groups often on opposite sides of the bargaining table, and it was not produced without conflict. *Variety* reported that the release of this document was delayed due to disagreement over the elimination of jobs. The AMPTP wanted to eliminate jobs to keep crews small, while the unions wanted to protect members' employment opportunities.[36]

The twenty-two-page white paper offers a wide range of tips for minimizing spread, including an overview of ways to physically distance, changes to set practices, and expectations regarding sanitization. Like the Georgia guidelines, the document offers broad general advice; for example, rather than mandating a testing schedule, it recommends "regular, periodic testing of the cast and crew," which leaves decisions about surveillance testing open to interpretation and application.[37] However, the task force is explicit about set hierarchies and *who* should be in charge of making decisions about safety and compliance, which is usually the unit production manager (UPM), or in other cases the newly created position of the COVID-19 Compliance Officer. This plan allows for a degree of flexibility in the application of different procedures, but in keeping with the hierarchical structure of set culture, it also establishes a chain of accountability.

Explanations of diagnostic testing, handwashing protocols, and the duties of COVID-19 Compliance Officers are all new additions to set procedures, but changes to craft services and physical distancing guidelines reflect the greatest cultural shift on set. In order to accommodate six-foot distancing guidelines, the white paper suggests that those who are able should telecommute and set meetings and writers' rooms should move to Zoom. Craft services, which frequently offer opportunities for conversation and camaraderie during breaks, also had to enact several key changes: buffets are eliminated, meal times staggered, and cast and crew must distance themselves while eating. In an industry often defined by its collaborative and social environment, these strategies are poised to fundamentally reshape set culture.

Although the white paper is a collaborative document, the unions had various points of contention with its implementation. Almost two weeks after the initial release of the plan, the unions released an additional document called "The Safe Way Forward" that expands on the white paper's protocols with some additional "organizing principles." Although the unions express that the "granular detail that lies beneath can be tailored to each production," the guidelines in this document detail the importance of testing, further define the role of the health safety supervisor and his or her teams, and offer specific departmental protocols.[38] While some of the core ideas about distancing and reducing numbers on set remain unchanged, "The Safe Way Forward" places less emphasis on sanitizing and more attention on testing. "The Safe Way Forward" also notably introduces what it calls a "zone system." This system divides the set into three regions: Zone A, which contains essential crew and actors, who cannot work with PPE; Zone B, which is the set surrounding Zone A, where crew members are appropriately distanced and wearing PPE; and Zone C, which consists of the off-set world. According to the guidelines, each zone requires different testing protocols. This system does not dramatically change the jobs of cast and crew, but it does create a system of labeling that requires workers to think about where they are and where they need to be. Compared to the industry white paper, this document adopts a more persuasive tone and uses more supporting evidence from scientists and medical professionals.

With the guidance of the white paper and "The Safe Way Forward," by mid-June Hollywood leadership had two sets of guidelines to resume production. Yet the industry did not reach an agreement for restarting production until September. Between the release of the plans in June and the final restart agreement, health experts had learned much more about COVID-19 transmission. By July experts clarified that COVID-19 is spread by aerosols, that surface transmission is unusual, and that temperature checks are unreliable because infected individuals do not always show symptoms. Thus, plans that emphasized surface cleaning and frequent temperature checks were seen as flawed, offering a false sense of security. The zone system outlined in the union plan appeared to be the most appropriate method to stop the spread of the virus. The effectiveness of "The Safe Way Forward" was reflected in the final agreement between the AMPTP and the unions, which adopted frequent testing and the zone system as foundational aspects of their return-to-work plan.

Hollywood unions and guilds are experienced at assessing set conditions, adjusting work hours and breaks, and negotiating for safe practices, but these pandemic discussions were unique because they required a radical reimagining of who can be on set and how that should be decided. Cast and crew often have specialized and long-established roles and respect on-set hierarchies. Return-to-production documents proposed new roles and reinvented some set practices that will shape the creative conditions and aesthetics of film and television for the foreseeable future. The new plans alter the social environment of the set and limit contact between workers. When we watch and reflect on the media produced during the pandemic, we need to consider how restricted access to set, the zoning system, and new safety supervisors all shaped communication, as well as the cultures of creativity that are the foundation of Hollywood productions.

PRODUCTION: LOOKING FORWARD

Around the world, studio and network leadership, union leadership, and directors and showrunners all worked to find ways to restart production as quickly and safely as possible. Film and television productions have always been attentive to safety concerns, especially as they relate to use of equipment and stunt work, but during this pandemic "safety" has to include physical health and protection from air-borne illness. In broader terms, one of the big questions for the postpandemic era will be whether or not people and employers continue to be concerned with illness and preventing the spread of transmissible viruses as part of wider safety concerns. Current science-based safety measures and expensive testing plans are not infallible. Despite safety protocols, productions have been continually hampered by COVID-19 outbreaks on set. For example, shooting on *The Batman* paused after only three days when Robert Pattison tested positive, while *Jurassic World: Dominion*, a production that administered 27,000 COVID-19 tests between July and mid-September, shot for thirteen weeks before eventually pausing due to an outbreak in October. These examples reveal little proof that Hollywood can completely manage exposure to the virus even with all its new safety practices.

COVID-19 protocols will certainly be in place for the duration of the pandemic, which was far from over at the time productions resumed in late summer and early fall. The consequences of these protocols are prolonged shooting schedules and inflated budgets to accommodate the expenses of COVID-19 safety measures. Major studios have reportedly been financing thousands of tests on big-budget shoots like *Jurassic Park: Dominion*, which added as much as $3 million to an overall budget. The prospects for independent films are entirely different. Studios and networks have the advantage of economies of scope and scale: decades of unchecked mergers allow them to shoulder losses in one division because they can be recouped by stability and success in other divisions, such as streaming or gaming (which also surged during the spring and summer months).[39] Independent productions are more vulnerable in the pandemic climate because they have fewer safety nets to shoulder losses, cover added expenses, or permit two-week pauses due to outbreaks—especially without production insurance. These conditions make large productions more viable during this pandemic. While this does not necessarily entrench the dominance of tentpole film culture in US cinema in the long term, it will likely result in fewer independent films getting made and released in the aftermath of the pandemic.

The prolonged pandemic in the US gave creatives time to acclimate to new production practices, procedures, and budget realities. Although there are many who will be happy to look back at the shows and films made under pandemic circumstances as unique time capsules of the period, some of the practices implemented to address health concerns will have a lingering effect on production. Changes to how content is made have already resulted in more animated projects and other big-picture production decisions that eliminate variables or opportunities for infection on set. The producers of *Zoey's Extraordinary Playlist* have talked about the importance of building sets (rather than using locations) to help create a more controlled environment. P. T. Anderson's latest film reused extras for multiple scenes to reduce the number of COVID-19 tests administered each week and to minimize on-set exposure. Other producers have turned to technology to reduce the number of people involved in production. For preproduction, VR technologies help scout locations and eliminate travel. During production, technologies such as Industrial Light and Magic's StageCraft (which was created for *The Mandalorian*) and Epic Games's Unreal engine enable producers to build out virtual settings that allow smaller crews to shoot scenes on heavily digitized sets.[40] For those working on film and television, the crucial question moving forward will be whether these innovations and changes to the production process have a long-term impact beyond the exigencies of the pandemic.

Union concern about unemployment shaped some of the negotiations and collaboration over return-to-work strategies in the early stages of the pandemic, but those were not the only important union decisions or negotiations that took place in the media industry in 2020. In August SAG-AFTRA announced that it planned to raise the minimum salary eligibility requirements (and exclude residual earnings from annual totals) for their health plan. Union leadership explained they needed to address financial deficits, but this decision, which would cause almost twelve thousand performers to lose their health benefits during a pandemic, angered actors, who filed a lawsuit against the union in December. The above-the-line unions all renegotiated their contracts amid widespread shutdowns. Prior to the pandemic there was speculation that the 2020 negotiations would be particularly fraught given that the Writers Guild of America was already in the middle of a dispute with agencies over packaging fees. Needless to say, widespread shutdowns due to a global health and financial crisis eliminated union strike leverage. There will be consequences from the rushed pandemic negotiations that ensued, even if they seem distant or abstract in comparison to prevention protocols on set, the shattering of release windows, or new seating capacities in movie theaters. The immediate focus for all of the unions was to find a way for the industry to get back to work, but contract terms provide an important baseline for future negotiations. In the first nine months of 2020, industry leaders and workers were focused on simply surviving the present crisis, but changes to union benefits and contractual precedents that these negotiations established will have lasting impact beyond 2020.

CHAPTER 2

DISTRIBUTION

WHEN THE PANDEMIC shut down production and theatrical exhibition venues in March, people around the world turned to Netflix. Of course, Netflix was not the only way people stayed entertained during the pandemic, but with its steady stream of new content, it represents one of the biggest changes to distribution in the twenty-first century—changes that were already well established when the pandemic hit. The many iterations of video-on-demand (VOD) rentals and electronic sell-through systems have been familiar to film studios and production companies for the past fifteen years. Similarly, television producers and networks had been acclimating to the effects of streaming media for over a decade. Although the technologies and methods of digital distribution predate the pandemic, what is new is the extent to which the film and television industries have had to rely on these services and the degree to which VOD and streaming, rather than broadcast and cable, dominated our viewing during this period of shutdown.

Distribution is not simply a technological process: it involves vast human networks, interactions, and infrastructure. As Alisa Perren explains, it typically includes "assembling financing, procuring and/ or licensing rights for projects for various platforms . . . , managing the inflow and outflow of income from various corporate partners, designing release schedules and marketing strategies to establish and sustain marketing awareness, and building and managing libraries."[1] In essence, distribution encompasses almost every part of the process that helps get films and television programming in front of audiences.

Historically there has often been a physical component in distributing 35mm prints of films or tapes, but in contemporary Hollywood, distribution often refers to many heterogeneous and immaterial practices, including the business of streaming services, the commerce and marketing functions of film festivals, and studio strategies for theatrical releases.

The pivots of 2020 precipitated by the pandemic were concurrent with some long-anticipated changes, which made for a particularly dynamic industry climate in the first nine months of the year. Digital technologies were essential for every aspect of distribution during the pandemic: new streaming providers sought to strengthen their services and stand out in a crowded digital marketplace; the in-person aspects of distribution deal-making had to move online; independent filmmakers were left frustrated with festival options; and studio chairmen and presidents found themselves desperately trying to salvage the summer movie season by distributing films on streaming platforms or as PVOD releases. These challenges were not entirely new to the industry, but the disruptions caused by production shutdowns accelerated changes in distribution practices at a bracing pace. Changes to release dates and marketing strategies were announced as temporary solutions during extraordinary times, but given that the media industries had been reorienting their business toward streaming services prior to the pandemic, promises of a swift return to prepandemic practices sounded dubious, especially to concerned exhibitors.

SHELTER IN PLACE AND THE
NEW STREAMING LANDSCAPE

In 2019 the US launch of Apple TV+ and Disney+, along with the impending launch of HBOMax and Peacock, marked the beginning of what trade reporters were calling the "streaming wars." Increased competition in the streaming landscape was predicted to reshape the media distribution landscape. Legacy media companies such as Disney acquired 20th Century Fox in 2019 in order to expand its film and television catalogues in anticipation of the Disney+ launch. Huge changes loomed on the horizon as film studios and television networks geared up to compete with established streaming services, including Netflix, Amazon Prime, and, to a lesser extent, the Disney majority–owned Hulu. The timeline for new services was well established long before COVID hit: launch dates were set, premiere parties scheduled, large sums spent on licensing fees for popular programs, and splashy new programming was announced. However, like all timelines and intentions in 2020, COVID-19 swept across the world and upended many plans.

While the first wave of streaming service providers were primarily tech companies challenging Hollywood from the outside, the newest streaming services are predominantly from legacy studios and networks, launching what are effectively extensions of existing broadcast and cable networks as apps, such as Disney+, HBOMax (WarnerMedia), and Peacock (NBC Universal). In addition to these library-heavy services, Apple launched Apple TV+ and Jeffrey Katzenberg (former CEO of Disney) launched the ill-fated and short-lived Quibi, which aimed to compete with TikTok and YouTube with premium mobile content for commuters. All of these services launched in 2019 and 2020 still trail behind Netflix, and many (except Disney+) lag behind Amazon Prime and Hulu, which have long-term subscribers who have grown accustomed to a constant flow of new film and television content throughout the year—not according to traditional film and television schedules and seasons.

Success for streamers during the pandemic has largely been based on where they were in their corporate timelines for launching services, brokering deals with carriers, and producing new content. The pandemic should have been an unexpected boon for home media providers, as shelter-in-place orders drove many to spend more time at home streaming films and television shows. However, the various streaming services experienced the effects of the pandemic in uneven ways. During the pandemic, the most globally focused streaming services, Netflix and Disney+, emerged with the biggest gains in subscriber numbers. When streamers announced their subscriber numbers alongside quarterly earnings in July, Netflix reported over 190 million subscribers worldwide, and Disney reported 60 million subscribers. Peacock launched in July with a promising 10 million subscribers, while HBOMax—which launched in May, was unavailable on Roku, and met with considerable consumer confusion about how this service differed from other iterations such as HBO Now and HBO Go—had a disappointing 4.1 million subscribers.

These streaming services created many more options for at-home audiences, and in 2020 audiences continued the practice of cord cutting and shifting between different content providers.[2] Cable providers, which have consistently passed along the increase in carrier fees to subscribers, saw a record 1.7 million subscribers cancel their packages in the first quarter and similar losses of 1.5 million in the second quarter.[3] For much of the summer streamers also had to contend with the rising churn rate, or percentage of subscribers leaving streaming services. Since many of the new streamers launched with free trials, analysts noted that the churn rate was 6 percent higher during the summer of 2020 than the previous year. The specific churn rate data for each service was unavailable. *Deadline* reported that the consulting firm Parks Associates simply explained that established services (Netflix, Amazon Prime, and Hulu) had lower churn rates, and high-cost streamer TV bundles had higher churn rates.[4] For many subscribers, the price of a Hulu+ Live TV bundle seemed excessive once live sports programming went on indefinite hiatus in March. While many services continued to accept churn as part of doing business, Disney+ eliminated its free trial in June, just prior to *Hamilton*'s release, with Netflix following suit and eliminating its free trial four months later.

With theaters shut down, streamers reaped the benefits of many films moving straight to streaming services. Films such as *Lovebirds* and *Palm Springs*, intended for theatrical release, slowly found their way to streaming platforms. In other cases, companies such as Disney scheduled early releases for attention-grabbing projects like the *Hamilton* film, which was originally slated for a 2021 theatrical release. Although audiences had access to new content, production shutdowns and delays hindered the release dates for many titles, especially television shows, which tend to operate on quicker timelines than films.

Library content was essential for streamers to sustain subscribers during the pandemic. In the domestic US market, streamers found that their libraries and licensed content became more valuable than ever. In the midst of the pandemic, Netflix, Amazon Prime, Hulu, Disney+, HBOMax, and Peacock benefited from their exclusive content acquired through prepandemic production, licensing deals, prepandemic mergers, and library acquisitions. By May, Apple TV+, which had attempted to rely solely on new content to attract subscribers, found itself on the lookout for content libraries to bolster their limited offerings. Analysts and journalists had anticipated that the "streaming wars" would be a battle over subscriber numbers. Instead, the unveiling of streaming services in 2020 seemed to be a series of somewhat disconnected battles: Netflix continued to try to expand its global reach, while Disney focused on Disney+ as a way to recover losses from other divisions. At the same time, the disappointing numbers for HBOMax confirmed the belief that library content alone is not enough; streaming channels need enticing new releases.

NETFLIX: LEGACY STREAMER

Six years after it initially began offering streaming content, Netflix licensed *House of Cards* in 2013 as an original series. The series ushered in a new phase for the company as it shifted from distributor to producer. The show, a remake of a popular British series, was a splashy first production, with episodes directed by acclaimed director David Fincher and starring Academy Award–winning actor Kevin Spacey. Although this show was ostensibly meant to attract new subscribers, its primary purpose was to ensure that Netflix would have its own exclusive content library—a collection of films and episodic shows it owned or controlled through long-term exclusive deals—and would not be stuck overpaying to renew licenses for content owned by other studios or networks. As media historian Eric Hoyt has demonstrated, the monetary value of film libraries has changed throughout history.[5] In the streaming era, conventional wisdom holds that new content is essential to attract audiences, but libraries offer a competitive advantage by providing catalogue depth. In business terms, this approach combines the long-tail model favored by tech companies with the blockbuster model common among legacy media companies: selling large numbers of inexpensive niche products but anchored by big, splashy content both old and new. As Michael Smith and Rahul Telang point out, the long-tail model was never going to replace the blockbuster model, but the processes of long-tail distribution offered a new way of distributing media.[6] Although Netflix began as a distribution service, its current strategy is to offer a large catalogue of licensed content paired with buzzworthy originals. In order to rapidly build a library and meet the constant demand for new content, Netflix has operated on a year-round production and release schedule. This gave Netflix a competitive edge during the shutdown, since it had many titles nearly ready or ready for release in 2020. It was able to continuously release new films and shows when other content providers were brought to a halt.

Netflix thrived during the pandemic as the company maintained a consistent stream of new releases as well as offering popular licensed content, not only in the United States but also for an increasingly global audience. As industry scholar Amanda Lotz notes, the focus on the "streaming wars" in the press has overemphasized the competition for US audiences and diminished the importance of global reach.[7] Lotz, Ramon Lobato, Jean Chalaby, and others have demonstrated that satellite networks and streaming services are most successful at courting international audiences when they produce localized content that caters to each marketplace.[8] While many streamers worked to bolster beloved Hollywood offerings, Netflix continued to broker deals with non-US production companies and build their global presence. Although the pandemic delayed production in many parts of the world, thus preventing some countries from developing localized content, Netflix continued to find ways to grow its presence as a global company.

In 2020 Netflix opened a new office in France, a nation that has been deeply committed to supporting theatrical films even as streaming services grow in prominence globally. Netflix's strategies in France showcase other ways of establishing their presence via philanthropy and programming strategy. In France, as they did in several other nations (including the United Kingdom and India), Netflix donated $1 million USD toward relief funds for film and television production workers. In terms of programming, Netflix licensed classic films for French territories and bought global rights to a number of French films.[9] These films (along with many French television series) helped to bolster the streamer's French-language offerings worldwide at a time when streamers were all competing for new content. Although foreign-language films and television shows do not typically draw a large US audience, with some noteworthy exceptions such as *Parasite*, Netflix likely sees the US popularity of some of these titles as irrelevant, especially if they help secure global viewers. The Netflix interface often obscures the country of origin for its content, and non-English-language titles are integrated with English-language titles, contributing to the appearance of a greater depth of new titles.[10] Thus, these titles serve an important function on the service, even for those in the United States who never watch the non-US offerings.

As an established streamer, during the pandemic Netflix focused on maintaining US subscriber numbers while continuing to expand its global reach. Netflix, unlike legacy studios such as Disney, cannot rely on classic characters and content. The Netflix approach has been to develop localized content by working with production companies around the world and eventually establishing offices as the company becomes more entrenched. In the case of France, cultural presence was not strictly based on media production but also on establishing a greater sense of goodwill for a company frequently characterized as contributing to the demise of theatrical film.

DISNEY+: LEGACY MEDIA

Disney+ had a gradual rollout around the world beginning in November 2019. Thus, while Disney was in the enviable position of having established US subscribers and buzzy shows such as *The Mandalorian* prior to the onset of the pandemic, it still encountered a few snags in its global release. In India, Disney+ partnered with Hotstar and planned to launch in April with the start of the Indian Premier League cricket playoffs. In addition to aligning with the start of a popular sports tournament, Disney+ had also planned red carpet launch events in India and various European nations that were promptly cancelled.

Live sports, promotional events, and new content are all important to help attract new viewers. On top of that, Disney controls a deep vault of globally recognized and family-friendly library content. As Jaap Verheul argues, the "vault," or library content, "became our primary site of engagement with pandemic screen cultures."[11] Recognizing that new content was limited, streaming services vied for familiar and comforting film fare to boost their offerings. The demand for library content created a more competitive market for older films. *Variety* reported in August that the number of licensing deals increased 50–70 percent, and fees for these deals had increased 20–50 percent. As one analyst pointed out, this demand for content was driven by the need for streaming services to create "catalogue depth perception" in the midst of a pandemic. The perception of a large catalogue also provided reassurance that there would be ample viewing material, making the subscription worthwhile.[12]

Kid-friendly library content gave Disney+ an edge over other streaming services, especially while families were trapped at home, but it was not sufficient to cover the substantial losses in other divisions, such as the theme parks. After reporting losses for the first time since 2001, Disney made a number of decisions throughout the summer to bolster content offerings on the streaming service. In addition to announcing new straight-to-streaming programming such as *Hamilton*, Disney would also make the surprising announcement that it would send its big-budget, live-action *Mulan* to Disney+. (For more on the economic ramifications of this decision, see the section "*Mulan*" below.)

The decision to release *Mulan* after months of delays signaled Disney's intention to prioritize its streaming service. The release plan was noteworthy: unlike most of the programming on Disney+, *Mulan* would be available for an additional fee on top of the subscription fee. This PVOD model differed from other on-demand models during the spring and summer, where distributors released films on other pay platforms such as Amazon or iTunes. This is important from the perspective of Disney's streaming launch because it reflects a true return to a model of vertical integration that ended with the *United States v. Paramount Pictures* decision (often called the Paramount Decrees) in 1948. In 2020, just a few weeks after the Paramount Decrees were officially overturned, US viewers not only found more classic Hollywood films readily available, they also experienced a taste of the era: Disney produced and distributed their film to be exhibited via their own streaming service.

HBOMAX

From its launch in May, HBOMax seemed to be hampered by an array of issues destined to limit its subscriber growth. In 2019 Warner-Media announced that its new streaming service, incorporating the wide array of Warner library content, from classic films to popular network sitcoms, would be called HBOMax. Premium cable network HBO had long been associated with quality programming, and the network already had two existing apps: HBO Go (which was connected to a customer's cable package) and HBO Now (which was an à la carte app for those without cable). But the new streaming service's name—HBOMax—made it appear to be a similar service with more programming options. Although the name might seem to be a savvy, or at least cohesive, branding decision, this launch led to lots of consumer confusion. Many potential subscribers were unclear about the differences between the three services, so by the end of July, WarnerMedia had completely eliminated HBO Go and HBO Now.[13] Further exacerbating the problems for HBOMax, the service was unable to reach a deal with Roku, which boasts 46 million users, making it the most popular streaming device in the United States. Negotiations with Roku remained unresolved throughout the spring and summer, which hampered HBOMax's initial growth, but the deal was finally settled just in time for Roku users to sign up and watch *Wonder Woman 1984* during the holiday season and, perhaps most importantly, save WarnerMedia's fourth-quarter report.

Those who were able to find and access HBOMax discovered the service had fewer programming choices than initially announced. As part of the launch, HBOMax was touted to feature new content that would build off the streamer's extensive library and licensed content. HBOMax—which houses the Warner Bros. film catalogue, the Turner networks, the prestige television of HBO, and (by August) the DC Universe content—already had a significant library to attract adult viewers. Prior to its launch, the streamer made news with record-setting deals for *Friends* ($425 million) and *Big Bang Theory* ($500 million) to lure viewers away from Netflix. In addition to paying top dollar for these popular broadcast shows, HBOMax planned a *Friends* live reunion show to attract new subscribers. When Hollywood production stopped, the *Friends* reunion found itself subject to multiple delays as the producers held out until the show could be filmed in front of a live audience. Thus, while HBOMax won the bidding war over these popular shows, the pandemic interfered with its ability to leverage them into attention-grabbing original content. Attractive library content, as HBOMax's disappointing second quarter demonstrates, is not a sufficient draw for a new streaming service.

When HBOMax found itself unable to release some of its scheduled new content, the streamer floundered. Christopher Nolan's *Tenet* (a Warner picture) was already scheduled for a Labor Day release, and the heavily anticipated *Wonder Woman: 1984* seemed unmovable from the theatrical calendar. By the end of the summer, it seemed like WarnerMedia had already made its big announcements about 2020 releases and would not be able to compete with Disney+, which managed to move some of their release dates. Although WarnerMedia appeared to adopt a conservative "wait-and-see" stance in relation to its theatrical slate for the first nine months of the year, in December it shocked Hollywood with the announcement that *Wonder Woman 1984* would get a holiday release on HBOMax and that their entire 2021 theatrical slate would be released simultaneously on HBOMax and in theaters. Unable to make waves in the first nine months of the pandemic, despite all of their big licensing deals, WarnerMedia needed to present a clear vision for the next fiscal year to assuage shareholders—even if that meant infuriating talent.

During this historical period of production stoppages, libraries became increasingly valuable, but they were not a sufficient replacement for new content. Streaming services such as Disney+ and HBOMax have a competitive advantage with the depth of their libraries, yet for companies such as Netflix, which is focused on expanding global reach through locally produced content, these US libraries will be of limited value in the postpandemic world. While we have experienced the pandemic through the film vaults, as Verheul suggests, this strategy of pandemic survival and content curation is unlikely to be representative of streaming's future.

FILM FESTIVALS AND INDIES

For filmmakers whose films are chosen to screen at big festivals such as Sundance (held in January and February), South by Southwest (SXSW) (held in March), and the Cannes Film Festival (held in May), film festivals can be the first, and sometimes only, opportunity they have to watch their final film with a theatrical audience. As director and producer Judd Apatow puts it, SXSW offers a particularly unique experience because "when movies are in movie theaters it's pretty rare that the room is sold-out. . . . So to watch it with a thousand people is really fun[;] it's like a rock concert. People aren't just showing up to watch a movie, they're really pumped."[14] From audience buzz to getting booed at Cannes, the festivals provide publicity for films and potentially contribute to critical conversations and award projections at the end of the year.

Beyond their cultural and promotional functions, festivals attached to film markets also provide a venue for meetings about buying and selling distribution rights for finished films, negotiating foreign presales for films in development or production, and financing future projects. Writing about film festivals in 2015, Dina Iordanova points out that festivals do not simply facilitate distribution, they increasingly include activities "intended to foster production."[15] In essence, film festivals offer more than just a communal viewing experience—they surround business meetings integral to the production and distribution of film with glamorous publicity-generating live events.

The first case of COVID-19 in the US was identified on January 20, only three days before the start of Sundance and the launch of the film-festival calendar for 2020. Following the festival many attendees experienced COVID-like symptoms, leading some attendees and medical professionals to consider the film festival to be "the first petri dish" of coronavirus in the United States.[16] Given the shortage of tests available in the beginning of the year, there is no way to know; however, film festivals, which gather thousands of people in close quarters to mingle, network, and watch movies together, seem to offer ideal conditions for the spread of the virus. Although many speculated in May that coronavirus spread rapidly around Sundance, the January festival wrapped without any immediate concerns about the safety of film festivals over the course of the following months.

Concern about the SXSW festival, which brings together people involved in the tech, music, and film industries, began in early March, prior to the wave of sports and production cancellations later in the month. Tech companies, beginning with Facebook on March 2, were the first to cancel their SXSW plans. Over the next four days *Variety* announced an onslaught of tech companies, studios, labels, and individual stars all withdrawing, until SXSW cancelled the festival altogether on March 6. (The WHO declared COVID-19 a pandemic on March 11, 2020.) Because SXSW was one of the first major entertainment events to be cancelled by the time the shelter-in-place orders were implemented around the United States in mid-March, organizers were already discussing plans to move SXSW 2020 film premieres online.

Film festivals have become increasingly important events within the global film economy, but many of them also make significant contributions to regional economies. In 2019 SXSW reported that the festival's total economic impact for Austin was $355.9 million, so the economic losses for festival host cities can be significant.[17] While Austin is home to its own year-round production cultures and can boast a number of significant filmmakers, SXSW places the city at the center of film conversations in mid-March. Although festival organizers have been able to facilitate the marketing and film market components of festivals, these measures cannot recuperate the incalculable losses to regional economies that play host to the thousands of visitors that typically attend. The necessity of moving festivals and markets online underscores the importance of film festivals for low- and mid-budget film production and distribution. Shifting the business components online certainly benefited production companies and distributors, but the cultural and social experiences of in-person film festivals are irreplaceable.

SXSW

Amid the onslaught of companies and artists announcing that they would not participate in SXSW 2020, journalists and lawyers speculated about whether SXSW and the City of Austin would be willing to cancel an event that generates millions each year for the local Austin economy. Further, *Variety* reported that some of the trepidation around cancelling the festival arose from the fact that SXSW was not insured against a pandemic. Despite these financial concerns, on March 6 the City of Austin cancelled SXSW, and several days later festival organizers laid off one-third of their full-time staff.

In the days following the festival cancellation, filmmakers spoke out about their disappointment. As David Alvarado, one of the documentarians responsible for *We Are as Gods* (slated to premiere on March 15) explained, "To have labored on a documentary for three years and then find out the festival was cancelled on the same day you've finished—it was just devastating."[18] In addition to losing its world premiere, *We Are as Gods* lost an important opportunity for the film to find a distributor. With SXSW cancelled, organizers focused on trying to fulfill the festival's marketing function and enable distribution and future financial support for films.

SXSW's solution was to bring the festival online, a plan that was met with trepidation from filmmakers still seeking distribution. SXSW organizers partnered with Amazon to launch this online version of the film festival, although at the time the trades did not release details of the deal and simply stated that those opting to show their films in the virtual festival would receive a screening fee after the end of the festival. Following the announcement, filmmakers expressed concern about whether a digital festival release would prevent them from obtaining wider distribution in the future. Actor-turned-director Alex Winter explains, "As an artist, you're releasing more and more power the more people see the film without you being paid."[19] Winter's remarks are framed in general terms, but they are especially relevant under the conditions of the SXSW-Amazon partnership. Although festival films were only slated to play for a ten-day window, the films were made widely accessible to all audiences via a commercial platform (with or without an Amazon Prime membership). While this digital festival could perhaps provide the opportunity for word-of-mouth buzz, the failure to restrict access posed potential impediments for distributors, who might reasonably claim that a film had been too widely distributed to be financially viable. Film festivals often provide buzz and marketing, but equally important for distribution negotiations is the exclusivity of the festival release. Faced with festival cancellation, SXSW organizers framed their pivots as attempts to support the filmmakers slated to show their films in the festival setting. The digital festival gave films the opportunity to find an audience and to qualify for Independent Spirit nominations, but these compromises did not necessarily provide them with a comparable opportunity to find a distributor. Some films were acquired by content-hungry streamers, such as *Lovebirds*, which premiered on Netflix; other films, such as *You Cannot Kill David Arquette*, were acquired over the summer months; and others, perhaps waiting for an eventual theatrical premiere, remained undistributed.

CANNES

The Cannes Film Festival was slower to cancel. In contrast with SXSW organizers, Cannes organizers were unsurprisingly resistant to an online option given Cannes's stances regarding theatrical and online screening spaces. Although Netflix was working on ingratiating themselves with French audiences in 2020, the Cannes Film Festival maintained its position on the importance of the theatrical film experience. Theatrical exclusivity for films released in France is a full month longer than the gradually shrinking window in the United States. In years prior, protecting the integrity of the theatrical experience has manifested in public disputes between the festival and Netflix, as festival organizers found themselves consistently at odds with the streamer over its unwillingness to release its prestige films in theaters and then wait thirty-six months before releasing them on the streaming service.[20] Although debates about the importance of the theatrical experience have been waged around the world for years, the discussion has been more pronounced in France, where Cannes organizers banned Netflix from competition and audiences have been openly hostile to Netflix. For example, in 2017 audiences booed the studio logo at the *Okja* premiere (the last time Netflix entered a film in competition). This refusal to change policies regarding release strategies stems from different cultural understandings of cinema, and during the pandemic it has colored much of the decision-making. Thus, while shelter-in-place orders forced cancellations of festivals from SXSW to the Tribeca Film Festival, Cannes organizers took an extra week for their decision and opted initially for a postponement to June rather than cancellation.

However, by mid-April, as COVID-19 spread throughout Europe, the postponement inevitably turned into a cancellation of everything except the Marché du Film (Film Market). Organizers rejected the idea of a digital festival even before cancelling the 2020 festival: festival director Thierry Fremaux explained, "[For] Cannes, its soul, its history, its efficiency, it's a model that wouldn't work."[21] Those who had attended the festival in the past shared this sentiment. Writing about the announcement of the festival's cancellation, *New York Times* film critics A. O. Scott and Manohla Dargis reflected on the Cannes experience. Scott remarked on the quasi-religious experience of the festival saying, "Losing it feels like seeing a page ripped out of the sacred calendar"; Dargis focused on the social aspect of the festival and moviegoing, concluding, "It's about community, which doesn't exist when you stream Netflix at home while eating your Postmates delivery."[22] Cannes organizers, Scott, and Dargis all share an understanding that attending an international film festival is a way of participating in a uniquely important collective global cinephilia—an experience that is seemingly unattainable in other festival settings.

In 2020 it was easy to mourn the loss of many cancelled events such as Cannes, and articles such as those by Scott and Dargis contribute to upholding Cannes as a rarified space, its attendees as tastemakers and protectors of film culture. Reflections on Cannes contrast with those about SXSW, which focus on losses for individual filmmakers and the city of Austin as well as the business-minded pivot. The cancellation of Cannes was seen as a disruption in film history and a loss for global film culture.

While movie-going might be a sacred experience for audiences at Cannes, the film market is a different experience entirely. Launched in 1959, the Marché du Film is one of the major global film markets. The Marché officially became part of the festival in 1983 to offset the inauguration of several other large film markets, such as the American Film Market and the European Film Market, formed in 1981 and 1988, respectively. Whereas the Cannes Film Festival itself presents a curated selection of global prestige films, the film market is indicative of the broader array of global film quality and prestige. Writing a scathing critique of Cannes in 2001, consultant and journalist Roger Smith explains, "Outside of the 50 or so films selected by the Festival honchos . . . there are nearly 1,200 other films being shown somewhere in Cannes as part of the Marché du Cinema, most of them unspeakably bad and of interest only to low-end video distributors."[23] Smith's dismissal of the Marché seems largely based on the quality of films, but he fails to acknowledge that the Marché has always been the home of a broader swath of genre films. Notably, throughout the 1970s, the pornographic film industry dominated much of the business conducted at the Marché.[24] Although the festival showcases noteworthy films on the big screen, over a thousand films screen at the Marché du Film, and in 2020 many of these screenings unceremoniously moved online.

The Cannes virtual market became two parallel events: one organized by the big agencies and the other by festival organizers. Finance and content divisions of the major US talent agencies—Creative Artists Agency (CAA), William Morris Endeavor (WME), International Creative Management (ICM), and United Talent Agency (UTA)—launched A Demain Marché (See You Tomorrow Market), which featured twenty-six presentations to financiers and buyers at the end of June. These presentations featured an array of projects, including official selections such as Thomas Vinterberg's *Another Round* as well as films in preproduction seeking financing. Following the US agency announcement, Cannes organizers announced that they would launch a virtual version of their own Marché du Film. From the outside, it appeared that there were two competing markets, although organizers for both markets repeatedly explained that this was not the case.[25] The head of the Cannes market, Jerome Paillard, insisted that plans for a digital pivot had been in the works since February. US talent agencies had simply been the first to jump into action with an announcement and a plan for virtual presentations and meetings. The official Cannes virtual market was distinct because it offered virtual screenings for participants.

The festival was cancelled, but Cannes organizers successfully hosted and ran the virtual market. Paillard raved, "We received lots of messages from professionals telling us that it felt just like being in Cannes," while the Cannes festival president commented, "The quantity and quality of exchanges made it feel as if we were there, mingling around the Marché's stands."[26] On the one hand, it is unsurprising that a festival press release summarizing participation in the market was positive; on the other hand, given the festival's commitment to the in-person theatrical experience, some of the comments read as overly enthusiastic assessments of how the business component was translated.

Once a year in Cannes, the art and commerce of film cohabitate through shared event spaces at the Cannes Film Festival and the Marché du Film. For almost forty years the market was inextricable from the festival, but 2020 changed the relationship between the festival and market. Faced with obstacles to in-person gatherings, organizers had to consider the essential elements that constitute a film festival. In this case the Cannes organizers determined that the social aspects of the theatrical experience were more important than the simple act of watching a film. As such, they believed the prestigious competition could not be duplicated virtually. However, while art could be put on hold, the commerce of filmmaking needed to continue, whether in person or online.

SXSW and Cannes reflect two culturally different responses to the sanctity of the theatrical festival experience. The US festival organizers stressed the importance of making films accessible to audiences as well as buyers, whereas Cannes organizers emphasized the value of the theatrical experience, limiting participation in the online film festival, We Are One: A Global Film Festival, while focusing on maintaining one of the festival's business functions. Although both festivals were able to partially pivot, the online festivals did not provide the level of exclusivity that can generate excitement or the word-of-mouth buzz and marketing momentum that can help films stand out in the crowded streaming and VOD landscape.

WINDOW COLLAPSE

At the pandemic's beginning, Universal's March announcement that *Trolls World Tour*, the sequel to 2016's surprisingly successful *Trolls*, would skip a theatrical window and move straight to PVOD was the most hotly debated media move of the spring. Originally slated to hit theaters on April 10, *Trolls World Tour* was deep into its marketing campaign when the pandemic began to sweep through the United States. Rather than moving the release date, Universal opted to release the film on its originally scheduled weekend on PVOD through Amazon and iTunes. The move to forgo the theatrical window angered theater owners and prompted a wave of speculation about what this could mean in the future—especially in light of the new streaming services. Although this announcement was jarring amid the other disruptions of the pandemic, it should not have been *surprising*, since the industry has been experimenting with VOD releases since 2005.

Breaking release windows (the period of theatrical exclusivity that theater chains rely on to drive their business) was a volatile issue between studios and exhibitors. For exhibitors, theatrical exclusivity is a central tenet of their business; VOD, and now streaming options, pilfers their profits. The continued importance of the theatrical window for pricey tentpoles also gives exhibitors (especially the major theater chains) leverage to negotiate the box-office split with studios, which see the calculation over the best release strategy for a film to be a bit more complex. Writing about multiplexes in the 1990s and early 2000s, Charles Acland explains how many multiplexes were like miniaturized theme parks. Although many theaters have reinvented their spaces to emphasize comfort and high-end concessions, this is just the newest way for theaters to make movie going an event.[27] These efforts have been successful, in large part, as theatrical releases (more so than VOD and streaming) have been effective in creating a cultural zeitgeist for films, which is important for the studios that invest millions making and marketing spectacular "event" films. However, not all films have successful theatrical runs, which can be attributed to a lack of marketing or of broad appeal.

Studios have long felt that niche, smaller budget, or even flailing films could likely find more of an audience if they were allowed to move these films from the theatrical screen to the home screen before the end of the theatrical window. In 2005 Disney CEO Bob Iger explained in a *Wall Street Journal* article, "We'd be better off as a company and an industry if we compressed that window. We could spend less money pushing the box office and get to the next window sooner where a movie has more perceived value to the consumer because it's more fresh."[28] Comments such as Iger's have been of particular concern to exhibitors, who do not want to lose audiences to the home video market. Speaking to this issue in 2007 at ShoWest, a convention for exhibitors (now called CinemaCon), John Fithian, head of the National Association of Theater Owners (NATO), called contracting release windows exhibitors' "No. 1 issue."[29] Although exhibitors were concerned that theatrical windows had become shorter throughout the 2000s, the new variety of release strategies did not usher in a complete collapse of exclusive theatrical windows—especially for the blockbuster releases.

The pandemic created a shift in the balance of power between distributors and exhibitors. Faced with limited options to release their 2020 slate of theatrical films, studios were more open to considering PVOD releases for tentpoles and streaming releases for mid-budget films. Months earlier a Chinese company, Huanxi Media, made a similar decision to release its potential blockbuster film *Lost in Russia* via its premium streaming service. This decision was met with criticism in China and, like many of China's pandemic strategies, seemed to be predictive of future decisions in the United States. In light of theatrical shutdowns and worldwide orders to shelter in place, many studios saw a digital release—whether on a streaming platform like Netflix or Amazon Prime or as a PVOD release—as the only option to recuperate some expenses. Given historical experiments with VOD releases and the release of Chinese films on streaming services, it seemed logical that films slated for theatrical release would move online. What was noteworthy about the *Trolls World Tour* release was its $19.99 rental price (as opposed to *Mulan*'s $29.99 rental fee in September) and Universal's commitment to experiment with an on-demand release of this scale. For exhibitors, the stakes were high; if *Trolls World Tour* was successful as a PVOD release, this could be a slippery slope toward the collapse of release windows and the end of the theater business.

The idea that shrinking theatrical windows will destroy movie theaters is at the root of exhibitor anxiety over digital and streaming media, but this anxiety seems a bit misplaced: historically, VOD films have not been the types of films that excel theatrically. Distributor experiments with straight-to-VOD releases started with small, low-budget, and independent films. In 2005 Steven Soderbergh's film *Bubble* received a day-and-date release, meaning that it came out in select theatrical markets and was available on VOD services the same day. Although the film's box-office totals were extremely low ($200,000), 2929 Entertainment CEO Todd Wagner declared that its performance on VOD and its foreign presales made the film a success. With no public data to support Wagner's assertion, we are left to draw our own conclusions about the success of *Bubble*'s distribution strategy. Although this film's release introduced a new and reportedly successful strategy for distributing smaller films, it did not immediately inspire a significant wave of independent and low-budget VOD releases. *Bubble*, a $1.6 million movie starring two unknown actors, typified the scale of film that received shortened release windows during the early 2000s. Low-budget films and documentaries typically have small marketing budgets and need sufficient buzz to help attract an audience, which film festivals and theatrical releases can provide; however, they do not need to recuperate the tremendous costs of tentpole movies.

Trade reporting in *Variety* often highlighted different distributor experiments with windowing to showcase distribution as a film-specific strategy. Distributors who release films to VOD often have greater control over a film's data and thus can control the narrative around a film's release. With some day-and-date releases, distributors were interested in using box-office totals and surveys to prove that VOD did not disproportionately harm theaters. Of course, this is difficult to empirically prove with just predictive data or audience surveys. In 2011, after building positive festival buzz, distributor Roadside Attractions opted for a day-and-date release for *Margin Call*. Roadside Attractions reported exit polls that said that 98 percent of *Margin Call*'s audience was unaware that the film was simultaneously available on VOD.[30] The company then used this poll information to claim that VOD does not poach significantly from theatrical box-office numbers, even though this data says nothing about the VOD audience. (Would they have gone to the theater to see the film if VOD were not available?) Further, the data does not indicate whether any of those theatergoers would have preferred to watch the film at home, instead focusing on this almost unanimous and semipositive piece of information. Distributors also played with spontaneous decisions to shorten some windows, as the Weinstein Co. did with *Snowpiercer.* Reportedly, after watching the French box office drop considerably after opening weekend, Harvey Weinstein planned a multiplatform release that would move the film to VOD three weeks after its theatrical premiere.[31] In each case, the financial stakes remained relatively low and returns were modest, but these moves were successful enough to garner enthusiastic public statements about revenue.

Studios such as Warner Bros., Fox, Sony, and Universal experimented with VOD releases for *Unknown, Just Go With It,* and *Tower Heist* in 2011, which resulted in vocal frustration from theater owners, but the big studios largely looked on as independents experimented regularly with different release-window strategies.[32] Three years after the initial studio experiments, at the end of 2014, Sony Pictures Entertainment (SPE) tried a day-and-date release that had the blessing of many theater owners, although the circumstances were highly unusual. After North Korea declared the film *The Interview* an "act of war," a group called the Guardians of Peace hacked the studio and released internal studio documents and emails via WikiLeaks. As part of the crisis management in the wake of the hacks, numerous theater owners said they did not want to screen the film in theaters, so SPE decided to limit the theatrical window and release *The Interview* day-and-date, making it the first studio film to adopt this release strategy.[33] In the wake of SPE's decision, President Obama criticized the cancellation of the planned theatrical release on the grounds that it suppressed artistic expression and catered to terrorists' demands. According to SPE, the film made $15 million in online sales; although this was comparable to opening weekend box-office totals for previous Seth Rogen films, this was the last studio experiment with a major VOD release until the 2020 COVID-19 pandemic.[34]

In the first nine months of the pandemic, decisions and announcements about film releases were made on a case-by-case basis, but in the wake of theatrical shutdowns, film releases tended to fall into two different strategies: a PVOD release or a delay until 2021. With theaters closed, studios contracted the theatrical window for films released in early March. Spring 2020 releases such as *Emma*, *The Hunt*, and *The Invisible Man* quickly went online for a $19.99 USD rental. Although the PVOD option was logical for films that would have previously opened in theaters, only Universal opted to digitally release one of its major spring titles, the previously mentioned *Trolls World Tour*. Studios also made plans for their summer films. Two of Universal's biggest tentpoles for 2020, *Minions 2: The Rise of Gru* and *F9*, were immediately bumped to the 2021 release calendar. In contrast, Paramount and Warner Bros. decided to announce new 2020 dates for *A Quiet Place 2*, *Top Gun 2: Maverick*, *Wonder Woman 1984*, and *Tenet*, and Disney announced delays for *Mulan*.[35]

Similar to the VOD releases prior to *Trolls World Tour*, Universal released limited data that cast the *Trolls* release in a favorable light. Universal reported that the film made almost $100 million within the first nineteen days of its release, and the studio received 80 percent of that revenue as opposed to the 50 to 65 percent it would typically receive from theatrical exhibitors.[36] Although NBCUniversal CEO Jeff Shell was unwavering in his excitement about the film's success, several journalists and analysts were quick to point out that without global box-office numbers and a clear sense of the marketing budget, it would be difficult to evaluate the film's success. As journalist Kim Masters points out in the *Hollywood Reporter*, the lack of data for this film also presents particular accounting problems for actors who were to receive bonuses when the film exceeded $350 million worldwide.[37] Since digital totals are more opaque than the typical theatrical release, these new pandemic release strategies pose potential challenges for agents and talent monitoring a film's success.

VOD experiments have, at least implicitly, always been about helping studios and distributors gain leverage over exhibitors. Regardless of whether the *Trolls World Tour* experiment was financially successful, Universal's celebratory remarks worried exhibitors. Notably, their comments elicited ire from NATO and sparked a fight with global theater chain AMC. From the standpoint of distribution, studios demonstrated that PVOD releases were viable. Although analysts may have been skeptical of the total *Trolls World Tour* profits, it was enough to convince AMC to renegotiate theatrical windows with Universal in July. When (and perhaps if) AMC reopens, given its ongoing financial struggles, major studio films will have much shorter theatrical runs before moving to PVOD. Audiences will (eventually) return to the movie theaters, but we will return to a different timeline of tentpole releasing.

The collapse of theatrical windows in 2020 was a shock to studios' way of doing business, but these emergency VOD releases allowed them to take advantage of the expansion of streaming platforms and fifteen years of experimentation with VOD release strategies. Even amid pandemic closures and the new streaming culture of 2020, major studios were, with the exception of *Trolls World Tour*, initially slow to release films straight to VOD or streaming. The consequences of breaking release windows ripple throughout the film industry. Actors and other key talent often receive compensation based on box-office success; theatrical windows boost the ancillary markets that follow; and, of course, this period of exclusivity keeps movie theaters in business. However, as the pandemic wore on and began to peak again in July, optimism about a summer blockbuster season waned, and studios started to reevaluate their release strategies yet again.

MULAN

The PVOD release of *Trolls World Tour* was surprising because it was the first big-budget film to break its theatrical window, but the announcement about *Mulan*'s release to Disney+ signified a new stage of decision-making amid the pandemic and signaled an increased emphasis on streaming platforms within studio conglomerates. Disney's decision to release its newest live-action remake as a PVOD offering on the Disney+ platform further cemented exhibitor fears about the role of studio streaming platforms in the industry. Rather than solely using Disney+ as a home for library and straight-to-streaming content, Disney, it seemed, might be willing to use its platform to bypass the theatrical window and exhibitor fees—a move that could potentially be more profitable for the studio. With Disney's theme parks closed during summer vacation months, no summer tentpole revenue, and a second virus spike in July, the Disney juggernaut had to turn its attention to its recently launched streaming service. Disney's newly anointed CEO (and former head of Disney parks) Bob Chapek refocused attention to the streaming service. The decision to move *Mulan*, Disney's most expensive live-action remake, to PVOD was significant. Early in the year analysts had predicted close to $100 million for its opening weekend, making the film poised to be Disney's latest success.

Disney's experiment with live-action remakes of classic animated films started in 1996 with *101 Dalmatians*, but beginning with *Cinderella* in 2015, the studio began to release at least one live-action remake per year. A remake of *Mulan* was inevitable in the context of Disney's tradition of live-action remakes and Hollywood's newfound commitment to increasing diversity on and off screen. Helmed by a female director, based on a Chinese folktale, and starring a Chinese actor, *Mulan* seemed like it would check all the requisite boxes for domestic and global success.

Although *Mulan* was heavily anticipated and success seemed preordained in 2020, in the year preceding star Yifei Liu's support of the Chinese government had stirred up controversy. In August 2019, during a period of prodemocracy protests in Hong Kong, Liu expressed support for the Hong Kong police when she retweeted an image from the Communist Party newspaper the *People's Daily* that read, "I support the Hong Kong police; you can beat me up now." As a company that makes family-friendly films for a global audience, Disney (and its stars) typically avoid making explicit political statements. Liu received messages of support on the Chinese social media site Weibo for her endorsement of the Communist government and her implicit criticism of the prodemocracy protesters. However, on non-Chinese social media (Instagram, Twitter, Facebook, etc.) activists around the world launched a #BoycottMulan campaign, which was rekindled in Taiwan, Thailand, and South Korea a year later. In the immediate aftermath of the controversy, Liu was absent from the major marketing push that took place at D23 Expo, Disney's fan convention. Likely in hope that the story and the furor would fade, Disney offered no comment on Liu's post. As the film's planned release drew closer,

Liu took a more neutral stance on the Hong Kong protests in subsequent interviews. In one early 2020 interview with the *Hollywood Reporter*, she simply stated that the situation was "complicated."[38]

In advance of the film's release, some scholars of Chinese politics speculated that Liu's comments might actually boost *Mulan*'s box office in mainland China. Certainly, the trade reporting that followed the decision to postpone *Mulan*'s release in March could be characterized as enthusiasm for the delay. *Variety*'s Rebecca Davis turned to the Chinese social media site Weibo to highlight anecdotal declarations of relief from Chinese fans with comments like "Thank god!!!! Now I [*sic*] won't be spoiled" and statistics explaining that news of the delay had been viewed 630 million times.[39] Although Davis's article addresses some of the early controversy surrounding the film's star, she tells a story of excitement for the film's release, affirming many of the predictions of the film's potential for box office success—whenever it might be available on Chinese screens.

Historically Disney has privileged the theatrical release window for new-release movies and has withheld classic titles such as *Snow White and the Seven Dwarves* to profit from additional theatrical windows.[40] But there were signs in 2020 that, under the circumstances of the pandemic, the studio would consider other forms of release. As noted earlier, former CEO Bob Iger had been vocal about changing release windows in the past, and at the start of the pandemic Iger also teased the potential digital release of other movies on the calendar (without specifying which ones).[41] Additionally, Disney announced some early moves to streaming, including the critically maligned *Artemis Fowl* (released on Disney+ in June), potentially masking what could have been a significant flop for the $125 million film. Despite these early indicators that Disney might break release windows, CEO Bob Chapek continued to express support for conventional theatrical strategies, saying in May that "we [Disney] very much believe in the theatrical experience."[42] This statement indicates, that, at least in May, major titles (i.e., *Mulan*) would not move from the theatrical release calendar.

When coronavirus cases spiked nationally in mid-July, Disney initially announced that the theatrical release of *Mulan* would be postponed indefinitely. The announcement triggered a small downward spike for Disney's stock. Days later, on Disney's earnings call, Chapek announced yet another change: *Mulan* would instead premiere on Disney+ on September 4, although he gave no initial details about pricing. The film, which would be made available to Disney+ subscribers in the United States and in some foreign markets, would also get a theatrical release in China one week later. The timing of Chapek's statement about *Mulan*'s release and the announcement of a wider opening in China were bright spots in a potentially bleak earnings call that correlated with the worsening pandemic conditions across the United States. Although Disney would miss the US box office for *Mulan*, it would still open in the world's second largest theatrical market.[43] China was not the only country that reopened its theaters over the summer; by the first week of August nearly half of theaters around the world were reopened in some capacity. Although theaters were partially reopened around the United States during the *Mulan* announcement, theaters in major markets like Los Angeles County remained closed, and survey data demonstrated many US moviegoers were wary of returning to theaters. In order for the film to get a wide and simultaneous release to capture some of the theatrical market in the reopened theaters (including Russia, China, and South Korea), Disney had to embark upon what the *Hollywood Reporter* would call days before the film's release a "Historic Dual PVOD-Theatrical Journey."[44]

Unsurprisingly, Disney's announcement to release *Mulan* online in nations still under tight restrictions was met with anger from those exhibitors worldwide who had reopened. The head of the UK Cinema Association saw the announcement as a bad-faith act: not only did it deprive audiences of the opportunity to see the film in theaters, it also prevented theater owners from programming new and desirable titles on their recently reopened screens. In a more emotional response, one French theater owner posted a video of himself destroying one of the *Mulan* advertisements in his theater.[45]

After a summer of shifting release dates and anxious speculation across industry trades and popular magazines, reports on the PVOD experiment seemed to be lukewarm — and this despite a respectable critical response. As is common with VOD films, studios control the narrative of popularity and box-office totals without reporting many specific numbers. In the fourth quarter earnings call, Chapek simply said he was "pleased" with the PVOD experiment.[46] However, as at least one journalist commented, this PVOD experiment did not inspire Disney to release Pixar's forthcoming animated *Soul* as a premium addition; the studio instead opted to release it free on Disney+ on Christmas Day. Independent analyst Samba TV estimated that *Mulan* opened with $33.5 million over Labor Day weekend (which, if accurate, is more successful than *Tenet*'s $20 million theatrical total over the same weekend).[47] Regardless of the film's financial success, Disney's willingness to pivot its strategy and release the film digitally gave them greater power and leverage with exhibitors who may have previously seen them as committed to theatrical releases.

While Chapek could spin the digital release as a success, its global box office was a clear disappointment. *Mulan* opened to $23 million in China — trailing the popular Chinese war film *The Eight Hundred*. This was especially grim in light of the country's thriving box office, which had fully recovered by September. *Mulan*'s performance did not align with the excitement the trades seemed to be proffering about the film's release throughout 2020. The film reported around $66 million in theatrical box office worldwide, which was substantially less than it was predicted to make for its US theatrical opening.

Upon the film's September release, Disney and the trades blamed *Mulan*'s disappointing box office on politics. This time there was minimal focus on Liu's comments. Instead the emphasis was on the production's cooperation with Chinese government organizations and its ahistorical and depoliticized use of locations. Hollywood has long used location shooting and identifiable vistas both to create an authentic sense of place and to cater to global audiences who enjoy recognizing their local spaces and landscapes.[48] In the case of *Mulan*, aerial shots of dunes and widescreen compositions of military training against scenic mountains enhance the spectacular elements of what should have been a theatrical (or even IMAX) release. Director Niki Caro, producers, and location managers specifically scouted locations to incorporate Chinese landscapes, likely thinking about the visuals rather than the political or ideological resonances of the geography. The specifics of the locations came to the attention of audiences reading the "special thanks" section in the credit scroll.

The end of the film specifically notes the names of several Chinese government committees and groups associated with the internment of Uighur Muslims in Xinjiang. Thus, in the wake of the film's disappointing release, Disney also came under fire from a bipartisan list of politicians as well as global audiences who condemned the company for working with organizations known for committing human rights abuses.

While there might be many lessons in the release of *Mulan* about PVOD, the film also demonstrates the problems of meeting the demands of both US and Chinese audiences. Recent Disney films have attempted to capitalize on diversity and inclusion, but progressive positions in the United States on race and gender are not always shared globally.[49] Perhaps more relevant to the case of *Mulan* is the fact that the film failed to capture a Chinese audience, while the particulars of Liu's comments and the treatment of location shooting led to controversy for North American audiences. Although Disney aims for political neutrality as a means to cater to all audiences, this is increasingly difficult to achieve in the contemporary global political landscape.

In the case of *Mulan*—a film that began with a tremendous amount of scrutiny around its subject material, its star's geopolitical perspective, and the politics of representation—the PVOD release does not fully change the narrative of the film's failure, but it certainly complicates its legacy and provides alternative explanations for the flop. Despite the fact that Disney had been building its subscriber numbers on Disney+ over the summer, the company was still resistant to the PVOD release. And while its executives have opted for other digital releases during the pandemic, there has been no clear indication that Disney, which prior to the pandemic dominated theatrical box-office totals in the United States and around the world, will wholly abandon theatrical windows. Yet, this does not diminish the importance of *Mulan*'s PVOD and global theatrical release. The bold decision to release the film on PVOD may have been instructive for Disney as it focuses more intently on its digital platform, but the studio should also learn from the various missteps made representing and using Chinese culture in the making of the film.

DISTRIBUTION: LOOKING FORWARD

Media companies have been setting the stage for changes to distribution with the announcement of new platforms and apps, but the pandemic forced studios into more immediate and decisive moves to VOD and streaming releases. For legacy distributors, streaming platforms (and some of the programming) were developed to coexist alongside theatrical releases, allowing media companies to take advantage of both the long-tail tech model and their established emphasis on blockbuster properties. Although streaming platforms were not presented as a replacement for big theatrical releases, exhibitor anxiety around digital distribution meant that these new services were perceived as a threat that in turn provided distributors with increased leverage over exhibitors already fearful of declining theatrical attendance. There is little to suggest that these pandemic solutions have been successful enough to replace in-person film festivals or theatrical exhibition, but the unusual circumstances of the pandemic have given studios, networks, audiences, and exhibitors new ways of thinking about how media can be distributed.

Hollywood studios will continue to make big-budget tentpole films—especially in the near future, since studios have an easier time justifying (and covering) the added expenses created by COVID-19 measures. Although many studios have been upbeat about PVOD returns, they have not been reporting totals that come close to those of big global theatrical releases. In order for the theatrical model to change, studios would need to fundamentally reshape their budgets. Until there are radical changes on the production side, studio tentpoles will continue to dominate our multiplexes and IMAX screens. However, changes to release strategies for low- and mid-budget films are likely. The pandemic has given studios more flexibility to rely on VOD and streaming services and to shorten release windows, which they will be tempted to take advantage of for underperforming films (in the *Snowpiercer* model). This will likely be true for mid- and low-budget releases, even after vaccinations restore the prepandemic order of theatrical distribution.

Rather than looking at studios moving films to streaming as a radical break in time-honored business practices, shareholders should consider that moves such as Disney's announcement that *Soul* would premiere for free on Disney+ and WarnerMedia's announcement that its 2021 slate would premiere simultaneously on HBOMax and in theaters are attempts to offer stability. By changing distribution strategies, conglomerates can potentially recuperate costs and help to balance the record losses many of these companies have seen in other divisions. In the case of both AT&T/WarnerMedia and Disney, focusing on their streaming businesses also required corporate restructuring, which both announced in the fall. Restructuring corporate hierarchies will undoubtedly have a more significant and long-term impact than the decisions to release *Trolls World Tour* or *Mulan*, but in order to understand the changes to studio release plans we will need to see how these work in concert with the substantial return of theatrical releases in 2021 and beyond.

Distribution shapes what we watch as well as how and where we can watch it, but for the most part these processes are invisible to audiences. Many elements of distribution had already adapted to the arrival of streaming platforms and a diminished reliance on physical media, but when the pandemic further destabilized legacy practices—such as collective understandings of the importance of film festivals, traditional release schedules, and, most visibly, exclusive theatrical windows—many aspects of distribution moved to center stage. As Shawna Kidman observes, it is important to consider why and when the public is made aware of distribution infrastructures.[50] In 2020 we may have become aware of distribution practices simply due to the competitive landscape and the desire for streamers to distinguish their service in the market. As we emerge from the pandemic it will be important to consider the impact of new and heightened awareness of the differences between streaming services, the role of film festivals and release windows, and how this knowledge impacts industry decision-making and the media landscape.

CHAPTER 3

EXHIBITION

IN 2020 PEOPLE AROUND the world cancelled weddings, birthday celebrations, and concert tickets due to the pandemic. It became the year in which all events, from weekly rituals with friends to major life events, went on Zoom. Individuals found the accumulation of cancellations and delayed events upsetting, but for businesses that rely on events—from movies to weddings to concerts—the pandemic was a financial catastrophe. As nations and states gradually enacted pandemic regulations in the spring, the first measure many took was to ban large gatherings. In the United States, and especially in New York, where the pandemic was particularly virulent, these restrictions meant that Broadway theaters, nightclubs, performance venues, and movie theaters were among the first spaces to temporarily shutter.

The term "exhibition" encompasses the public presentation of media, whether online or in theaters, but the pandemic's effect on in-person theatrical business merits special attention. Theatergoing is an event, and as such many of our moviegoing practices were radically altered in 2020. When we think about going to the movies, we tend to imagine watching a film in a dark room with an audience. Even the language surrounding a film's financial success, the "box office," speaks to the location-specific experience of moviegoing. Around the world, exhibitors have focused on improving theaters by upgrading sound, screens, and seating, thus adding to the experience of moviegoing. While Thai theaters have innovative offerings like in-theater massage, most theaters have done this by adding high-end concessions and alcohol. Although John Fithian, head of NATO, announced in 2014 that alcohol sales were the "future" of movie theaters, Caetlin Benson-Allot has shown that alcohol consumption and sales are also very much a part of the history of exhibition.[1] In the prepandemic world, movie theaters had increasingly focused on ways to enhance the space and experience of theatergoing in ways that were, unfortunately, useless during the pandemic.

The variation in US responses around movie theaters foregrounds differences in state-by-state pandemic policies. While other sectors of the film industry were able to resume operations over the summer, movie theaters continued to struggle to successfully reopen, but the challenges they faced varied according to location. Some problems were global: the lack of new releases to attract audiences; the expense of structural upgrades to ventilation systems; and, perhaps most importantly, the reluctance of significant numbers of people to sit with strangers—who might be unwilling to wear a mask or are asymptomatic carriers—for two hours in an indoor space.

The industrial and economic story of movie theaters during the pandemic has been tumultuous, but the story of live venues has largely been tragic. In addition to the performers, staff members, and bartenders who make their living working live shows, companies like LiveNation and Ticketmaster, which provide the broader infrastructure around many of these businesses, furloughed and laid off thousands of employees. Established talent often was able to stay busy while sheltering in place: comedians like Mike Birbiglia organized virtual comedy shows like *Tip Your Waitstaff* to help support comedy club staff; and musicians on indefinitely paused tours came together for *One World: Together at Home* to benefit the WHO's COVID-19 Solidarity Response Fund. Over the summer, a luxury event and travel agency organized an exclusive Chainsmokers drive-in concert in the Hamptons with tickets going for up to $25,000. After the event, the attendees' social media posts revealed multiple social-distancing violations, and the concert was publicly lambasted by New York officials. Needless to say, it did not become a common model for other shows. Thus, while there were certainly some attempts to pivot live performances into pandemic-conscious formats, live venues had fewer viable solutions to create safe events and generate revenue.

The physical space is obviously a key part of the theatrical experience, but the social and collective aspects of moviegoing with our friends and neighbors are also essential. Theatergoing is at its best as a shared experience. Many of my moviegoing memories not only involve other people but also are shaped by that collective viewing experience: laughing at audience commentary with the crowd during Tuesday night Grindhouse at the New Beverly in Los Angeles; trying to contain tears along with 365 other people before the lights came up at the end of *Fruitvale Station*; feeling at home in a theater full of multigenerational groups of women before *Little Women*; and enjoying some of the regional and UGA-specific callbacks during a screening of *The Room* are just a few of my own memorable theatrical experiences. In a time with so much available media, films resonate differently, during viewing and after, depending on how and where they are watched.

In 2020 we were unable to watch movies in crowded theaters. However, theaters had to find ways to stay in business. Global theater chains like AMC as well as independent and arthouse theaters found an array of ways to adapt and even prepare for the future. They often did so by increasing retail offerings and trying to reproduce aspects of the theatrical experience. People also found ways to share their viewing experiences, whether it was at a drive-in, at home via a plug-in extension, or by actually going to the theater to see classic titles or new films like *Tenet* that attempted a theatrical release. Hollywood has lamented the decline of theatrical exhibition for decades, and, while the loss of the summer blockbuster season was clearly dire for theater owners, the pandemic did not quell the desire for collective viewing experiences.

THEATERS GO DARK

In late January 2020 Chinese officials announced that thousands of movie theaters would be closed in order to help stop the spread of the COVID-19 virus. Chinese New Year, the country's biggest box-office week, loomed on the horizon, making this a challenging economic decision. On January 23 the Chinese government closed thousands, though not all, of its 11,000 theaters (and 70,000 screens). By late February *Deadline* reported that analysts estimated China's theater closures had already resulted in a $2 billion loss to the United States' global box-office totals and that those losses would double over the following month if more theaters closed.[2] As cases began to spike globally in early March, theater revenue continued to decline. That was followed by the worst-case scenario: the announcements of more global theater closures.

Moviegoing is a social activity that takes place in an enclosed space, so it is natural that theaters were forced to close in a pandemic. Although it was clear that theaters should be closed, there was little consensus around the world regarding how long they should remain closed. China, India, and the United States all have robust domestic film production industries that fuel strong national box-office numbers, but their respective responses to theater closures reveal stark differences. China was notably on an earlier shutdown schedule than the rest of the world, and its theatrical closures were supported by strict quarantine practices and contact tracing. In India theater closures began in the northern region, but eventually theaters across the country were ordered, via national mandate, to close until June; reopening dates shifted several times over subsequent months. Similar to India, exhibitors in the United States were optimistic that many chains and theaters would reopen at the beginning of June. This reopening goal was partially realized due to a fragmented federal reopening strategy.

Theater owners around the world differed in their estimation of the costs and consequences of closures, but they could agree about the primary concerns going forward: In what form would theaters eventually be able to reopen? And what would they be able to screen?[3] Theater closures in the United States coincided with announcements of postponed summer releases. Around the world, repeated release delays were met with frustration from theater owners who feared that when they did eventually reopen, they would not have new and popular US tentpoles to attract audiences. Theaters in China, India, and the United States operate regionally, but they rely on national and global systems of film distribution. This limited some of their autonomy as businesses during the pandemic and presented unique challenges for reopening without Hollywood's summer movie slate.

CHINA

Throughout the 2010s, industry analysts and Hollywood trades speculated that China would eventually overtake North America as the world's largest theatrical market. China consistently reported the second-highest box office totals. The number of screens around the country continues to grow and now surpasses the number of theaters in the United States. Thus, when China shut down theaters during its most profitable moviegoing week in January 2020, the move caused tremendous concern for the profitability of its own domestic blockbusters, but it also troubled Hollywood studios, whose films frequently dominate the list of foreign films approved for theatrical release in China.

China was the first country to close theaters because of the pandemic and the first to attempt to reopen them. Unlike the US film industry, in China the state partially controls production, distribution, and exhibition, meaning the government has a public health interest as well as a vested financial interest in closing and reopening theaters. In late March, as COVID-19 cases rose around the world, they were declining in China. In response, the Chinese government allowed 500 theaters to reopen and announced that they would approve 205 more to open in the following week.[4] Theater reopenings lasted only six days before case numbers increased in parts of the country. Although the new cases were not specifically connected to theater attendance, the Chinese government reclosed all theaters across the nation. This quick rescission of the reopenings in China showcases one of the ways that a more centralized government was able to respond more efficiently and with greater force amid the global crisis.

While the first attempt to reopen theaters in China was unsuccessful, by July 20 venues began reopening again. This process was gradual; fewer than half of the theaters opened initially—and these in specific regions—and some theaters closed again immediately in response to regional outbreaks. A series of conditions were tied to theater reopenings. In the first stage, theaters resumed showings with older titles that would draw smaller crowds than the flashy block-busters. In addition, theaters were required to reopen at reduced capacity, to check temperatures of audience members, and to shutter concessions in order to ensure that patrons would keep their masks on during the film. Although China reopened efficiently in August and September, distribution of new US blockbusters remained delayed while theaters rolled out a backlog of US films from the previous year.[5] Thus, Chinese screens were dominated by Chinese films throughout the end of summer and early fall. These particular conditions have been a boon for Chinese films, which lead box-office totals in the domestic market. By the end of August, China's box office had completely recovered—sooner than any other nation—and had done so largely with domestic productions.[6]

INDIA

Unlike many countries in the world, India has a thriving domestic film industry (Bollywood) and continues to be less dependent on US media imports than many global markets.[7] In India's $2.7 billion media industry, Hollywood films account for only 13 percent of its revenue. Bollywood caters to an active moviegoing audience, with Indian theaters selling more tickets annually than China. The Indian film industry produces over two thousand films per year, making India the world's most prolific film producer. Although the industry is thriving, low ticket prices and inexpensive streaming services make India's robust media industry less profitable than the US or Chinese film industries. Nevertheless, its large media market makes it attractive to US studios and streaming services, which have tried to cultivate demand for US content. When the pandemic hit, Indian theaters followed shutdown practices that were similar to those in many other countries around the world. The March 24 announcement to close Indian movie theaters rolled out by region, and leaders initially believed that theaters would reopen by June. As was common around the world, this date was pushed back multiple times, and theaters were ordered closed until August 31, a date that also continued to shift as case numbers remained high in August. This was a familiar trajectory for many movie theaters around the world as countries struggled to stop the spread of the virus.

While theaters in India remained closed during the summer and fall, new features went directly to one of the many streaming services available to Indian consumers.[8] The streaming landscape in India comprises a mix of Indian companies and US-based global companies. Price is an important factor in streaming popularity—Netflix had been available in the country for a number of years, but it only became popular after launching a low-cost mobile plan.[9] In a market with many inexpensive streaming options, US attempts in 2020 to capture global revenue by releasing films on streaming sites faced challenges. Having launched Disney+Hotstar in April amid the pandemic, Disney was prepared to roll out new releases on its service. As Hollywood releases moved to streaming services, it became clear that Disney would need to release *Mulan* globally on Disney+ in markets where theaters remained closed, but as the studio later announced, *Mulan* would not premiere on Disney+Hotstar until December. The primary reasoning for this seems to have been that lower-priced subscription plans are not conducive to premium additions. In India, Disney's global PVOD pricing for *Mulan*, which was equivalent to the $29.99 USD price point, cost more than an annual subscription to Disney+Hotstar and would have been approximately ten times the cost for a single ticket to see the film.

Differences between the cost of viewing media in India versus the US and European markets present one of the core issues and obstacles for global streaming services in India. For streamers to be successful, they need to adjust subscription tiers and price points to be competitive in the market. Disney's experience with the release of *Mulan* further underscored some of the problems US streamers have had entering this market and pricing services appropriately. During a year in which theatrical revenue was unavailable, the challenges associated with acclimating to a new culture and market were costly.

THE UNITED STATES

As theaters closed in China and South Korea throughout February, US journalists and industry analysts were already asking what would happen if domestic movie theaters followed suit. By early March, CEOs of chains such as Cinemark and AMC implemented enhanced cleaning measures they had previously used during the SARS and swine flu outbreaks and decisively stated that they did not anticipate closing. Industry analysts seemed largely optimistic about domestic theater closures. While some forecasters were confident that theaters would stay open, the most pessimistic analysts speaking in the trades thought that while closures could happen in March, the end of 2020 might be more likely.[10] Although CEOs of the major chains were cognizant of the potential threat posed by the coronavirus, like many US businesspeople, they did not express public concern that it would spread as quickly as it did. But by March 19, the fears of mass theater closures were realized. In North America 96 percent of theaters shut down, which meant 4,900 theaters were closed until further notice, leaving audiences with 233 theaters and drive-ins remaining.

On the heels of theatrical closures, Disney and the box-office reporting agency Comscore announced that they were suspending box-office reporting. Since most theaters were closed, there was obviously little to report in March, but this offered a strategic advantage for studios. The absence of box-office data allowed studios to control the narratives around the success (and, more likely, failures) of streaming titles and of the few new theatrical films that found their way into theaters as they slowly began to reopen over the next several months. The pandemic resulted in financial losses on tentpole films, but in the long term the most important shift during this period was how studios restricted access to box-office data that tells part of the story of a film's popularity—and profitability.

Since the White House ceded all pandemic planning to individual states, reopenings of domestic movie theaters were as haphazard as they were for all other businesses. Theaters in Georgia were allowed to open beginning in late April but were not prepared for customers until May. Following Georgia, Texas movie theaters also reopened; more theaters in the southern half of the United States slowly followed suit by offering an array of screening options ranging from private bookings to limited-capacity showings. However, in states with stricter guidelines, such as California, indoor theaters stayed closed throughout the summer. Although over half of US theaters had opened by the first weekend of September, during the spring and summer there was no time in which all the venues were open.

Theaters worldwide—both major chains and independent theaters—struggled with pandemic closures. As businesses that are uniquely situated between global and national supply chains and national or regional restrictions, even those theaters that could reopen found themselves in a difficult position. Making the situation even more trying, some theaters, such as those in Massachusetts, found that when they were able to reopen, they were not allowed to exploit their most profitable revenue stream: concessions. Stuck in a precarious situation in which theaters had limited options, many owners were also watching as theatrical windows were shattered, leaving them with even greater uncertainty about what the postpandemic market will look like for their business.

GLOBAL THEATER CHAINS: AMC

When theaters closed worldwide in the first three months of 2020, theater owners were clearly concerned about short-term finances and their ability to stay open without income. However, for theater owners around the globe, as well as the members and leadership of NATO, the long-term ramifications of shortened theatrical windows were more troubling. Each time a studio sent one of its blockbuster films to a streaming service, theater stocks tumbled, indicating that Wall Street believed that this particular form of release-window disruption was unprecedented and had the potential to change the film exhibition business permanently. Although the Chinese box office recovered, the most significant issue for the United States seemed to be the duration of the pandemic, which stretched on throughout the summer, fall, and winter and left theaters with few new films and significantly reduced attendance. While all theaters struggled in 2020, the world's largest movie theater chain, AMC, which is minority-owned by the Chinese Wanda Group, teetered on the brink of bankruptcy. Throughout the spring and summer, AMC's problem-solving measures and negotiations set new terms for distribution and exhibition that promise to reshape the film industry in the postpandemic world.

AMC's prepandemic spending had put them in debt, which meant they were in a weakened financial situation when everything shut down. In 2016 AMC acquired several theater chains in the United

States, the United Kingdom, and Ireland and also began to renovate theaters and invest in recliners with the hope this would boost future business. In the short term, this investment in luxury seating meant that the chain took on a tremendous amount of debt in the years leading up to the pandemic. Although theaters lobbied Congress for loan guarantees and tax benefits as part of the CARES Act in March, these pleas were unsuccessful. Days after shuttering theaters, AMC announced mass furloughs for executives and employees alongside the news that they would stop paying rent on their theaters. As theater stock prices kept dropping, many financial analysts speculated that AMC's cash reserves were so low that the company would likely need to file for bankruptcy.[11] However, AMC was not out of options in April. There was some speculation that minority owner Wanda Group might help bail out the chain, and AMC was looking for ways to restructure its debt. However, with no end in sight for the pandemic, AMC, like many other theaters, both chains and independents, appeared to be in a precarious situation for the foreseeable future.

AMC's public struggles during the pandemic add another layer to the picture of why Universal's direct release of *Trolls World Tour* to streaming platforms (and drive-ins) was contentious. Many in the industry processed this sudden and surprising break with the release-window model in the context of the dire impact it portended on the future of theatergoing, but AMC was also concerned about its present solvency. Eighteen days after the film's release, Universal announced the returns on *Trolls World Tour* and declared the move a success. Universal CEO Jeff Shell was so enthusiastic about the numbers that in an interview with the *Wall Street Journal* he declared that postpandemic he "expected to release films in both formats [theatrical and VOD]."[12] Shell's remark that this strategy could become more common in the future sent shockwaves throughout the theater industry. Although analysts, journalists, industry leaders, and armchair critics had all speculated *for years* that studio films might increasingly go straight to streaming or PVOD and skip the theatrical window, Shell's declaration seemingly caught exhibitors off guard amid the pandemic. NATO issued a statement accusing Universal of being opportunistic, writing, "Universal does not have

reason to use unusual circumstances in an unprecedented environment as a springboard to bypass true theatrical releases."[13] Later in
the same day, AMC CEO Adam Aron responded with a statement to
Universal chairman Donna Langley: "Going forward, AMC will not
license any Universal movies in any of our 1,000 theaters globally on
these terms."[14] This provocative statement garnered headlines across
the trades and in mainstream news sources and inspired similar announcements from other chains promising to follow AMC's lead,
but, as a real threat, it was unlikely that AMC would follow through.
First, AMC would have to be willing to forgo the potential box-office
share of popular and eagerly awaited franchise installments like *F9*
and *Minions 2*. Second, Aron's letter repeatedly expressed a willingness to negotiate release windows. In the end, though, AMC's ulti-
matum did convince Universal to come to the negotiating table.

Universal's interpretation of the *Trolls World Tour* viewer data in-
stigated a long-overdue conversation about release windows. Universal and AMC exchanged fighting words in April, but over the next
few months there was limited conversation about whether AMC
would continue to ban Universal films or if the theater chain would
reach an agreement to allow the studio to shorten release windows.
Analysts speculated over who had the most leverage in the dispute
over the future of theatrical windows. While many pointed out that
studios have control because they control the content, others felt that
the importance of the theatrical box office for tentpole films gives
exhibitors the incentive to work together to strong-arm the studios.
With exhibitors weakened by the pandemic and studios embold-
ened by a greater number of streaming services and a robust array
of options for VOD releases, alternatives to theatrical release methods inevitably proliferated during the spring and summer.[15] As more
studios experimented with streaming releases, they began to collect
information and data about how feasible this process could be in
the postpandemic world. Regardless of the balance of power prepandemic, during the pandemic studios were well positioned as compared to hard-hit exhibitors who were merely trying to survive the
pandemic closures.

Ultimately when Universal and AMC announced their deal at the
end of July, release windows had shrunk, but AMC came away with

concessions that would support movie theaters in a world of additional streaming content. The Universal-AMC deal allows Universal the option to release its films digitally after a seventeen-day theatrical window (including three full weekends). After this theatrical run, Universal can release films as PVOD for around $20. Although this marks a significant change to the previous ninety-day theatrical window, it does not mean that Universal will opt to release successful theatrical films as PVOD after seventeen days. Thus, it is unlikely that we will continue to watch tentpole films in our living rooms or on our computer screens in the postpandemic world. Ultimately theatrical runs are more lucrative and have historically been essential to generate the kind of buzz that creates demand for sequels, toys and other ancillary merchandise, and theme-park rides for Universal Studios parks. This change in windowing does, however, allow Universal to shift an underperforming film to streaming and to have greater control over the narrative surrounding the film as a success or a flop. In addition to changing the windowing requirements, AMC also negotiated a percentage of the PVOD profits, which would help ease the blow of shortened theatrical windows.

The AMC-Universal deal was monumental, but officially it only affected one theater chain and one studio. But in negotiating their own deals, major theater chains like Cinemark and Regal would need to contend with AMC's precedent-setting terms. In the immediate wake of the deal, Cinemark CEO Mark Zoradi expressed the opinion that it was premature to renegotiate theatrical windows. Zorandi clarified some of his critiques, saying, "An aggressive shortened theatrical window could have an adverse impact on the mid-to-tail end of a film's life."[16] For exhibitors in the prepandemic world, moving a film to VOD late in its theatrical run amounts to lost ticket and concession revenue.

While the CEOs of large theater chains expressed disappointment in the deal, the responses from independent theater owners ranged from dissatisfied to fearful of the future. *Variety* reported that some independent theater owners were afraid of being blacklisted by studios and were unwilling to go on record with their critiques of the AMC-Universal deal. Others, however, believed that this change was both inevitable and necessary to push theaters to change their practices in this new media landscape.[17] Producer Jason Blum and at least one Atlanta theater owner believe that shortened windows might make studios more willing to give a greater number of films a chance at a theatrical release, thus creating a more diverse array of big-screen options in the future.[18] Regardless of where CEOs and owners stand on this spectrum, all acknowledge that the Universal-AMC negotiation set a precedent that would eventually shape the postpandemic movie world.

By the end of the summer, as AMC realized, reopening theaters in the United States did not equate to a return to normal operations. Select AMC theaters opened in August in those southern states under more lax social-gathering policies. In celebration of AMC's one-hundredth birthday, the chain announced a promotion: select theater locations would be opened with fifteen-cent tickets for classic titles; tickets would later go up to five dollars. This soft reopening featuring classic titles was well timed for theaters to practice protocols in advance of the September release of *Tenet*. However, the August discounted pricing was heavily criticized in an article in the *Los Angeles Times* that accused AMC of preying on low-income families who would presumably find both of these discounted price points hard to resist: the promotion might ultimately serve to spread the coronavirus. The article, which is classist in its rhetoric, also did not demonstrate any understanding of differences in national ticket pricing (many theaters in the South regularly offer $5–6 tickets for new movies on weekdays) and painted a sensational image of AMC's reopening marketing ploy.[19] While the fifteen-cent tickets seemed to be an attention-grabbing move for AMC that also gave their stocks a boost, it did not ultimately entice moviegoers back into theaters.

AMC was the first theater chain to open up negotiations about theatrical windows during the pandemic, and as such, the company is specifically implicated in the broad changes to theatergoing practices and cultures. Undoubtedly these negotiations were born out of unprecedented stress on the theatrical sector: like many businesses reliant on in-person events, AMC struggled. Subsequently, AMC's path to reopening—which included implementing new precautions, a slow initial reopen featuring classic titles, and, finally, reduced-capacity screenings—resembles the one taken by many theaters in

2020. Although the path for reopening individual AMC theaters was unremarkable, the company contributed to one of the more significant policy changes of the pandemic by initiating the collapse of studio windowing. Between reopening and the Universal negotiations, CEO Adam Aron proudly and perhaps naively announced that AMC, after restructuring its debt in July, closing several theaters around the United States, and rolling out a reopening plan, had "survived the corona crisis."[20] In subsequent months, following *Tenet*'s lukewarm box office and case spikes in college towns, it became clear that there were other struggles ahead for the movie theater industry.

US ARTHOUSE AND INDEPENDENT THEATERS

From Wuhan, China, to Athens, Georgia, movie theaters are the physical locations where people connect to Hollywood. Movie theaters also employ people in small towns and large cities as part of regional economies. Thus, while they are subject to Hollywood decision-making, they can also be a small business or a nonprofit that is integral to the livelihood of employees and the culture of a town.[21]

Georgia was the first state to reopen businesses in late April, and movie theaters (along with salons, massage parlors, tattoo parlors, and bowling alleys) were part of that first wave of reopening. Reopening businesses in the United States was a divisive political issue during a particularly polarized year. In a purple state like Georgia that is divided into 159 counties, reopening plans aligned with county politics. Republican governor Brian Kemp clashed with Democratic mayors in cities and towns (such as my hometown of Athens) who advocated, often unsuccessfully, for stricter guidelines. Athens, however, is divided between one predominately Republican county (Oconee) and one Democratic county (Clarke). Thus, when reopening happened, many Clarke businesses remained closed or reopened with strict restrictions, but one only had to cross over into neighboring Oconee County to find bustling businesses.

The closures affected all regional movie theaters, but neither the effects nor the survival strategies were the same. While the scope and scale of the global chains (AMC, Regal, and Cinemark) initially offered those theaters some degree of protection, smaller independent chains, which the NATO defines as any chain with seventy-five or fewer screens, and solo arthouses had to find other strategies to generate income and retain a presence within their respective communities. Over the course of the summer, theaters relied on professional organizations like NATO and Arthouse Convergence, which martialed financial resources and helped owners strategize virtual solutions and create eventual reopening plans.

Theaters around the United States and the world navigated closures and reopenings, but this is the brief story of two theaters in Athens, Georgia. Before the pandemic started there were four movie theaters in Athens: an AMC (which permanently closed in late September); two multiplexes (Beechwood and the University 16) that are part of the employee-owned Georgia Theater Company (GTC), which consists of twenty-two theaters statewide; and the nonprofit arthouse in downtown Athens, Ciné. Speaking to the challenges of staying afloat during the pandemic, John Fithian quipped, "Nobody starts a GoFundMe for an AMC. Although I wish they would!"[22] Although all theaters faced the same challenges of limited films and severely reduced attendance, Fithian's comment speaks to the different fundraising options between chains and beloved local independents. Each movie theater contended with the early reopening in different ways. The AMC remained closed in compliance with corporate policies, the GTC sought to follow NATO professional guidelines for safe reopening, and, throughout the summer, the board of directors and executive director of Ciné kept the theater closed while exploring different ways to generate revenue. As a chain, the GTC theaters relied solely on ticket sales for income and reopened (to varying degrees) throughout the spring and summer, but Ciné, which is a nonprofit with solid community support and cultural cachet in Athens, remained closed into the fall.

GEORGIA THEATER COMPANY

Governor Brian Kemp announced that select businesses were allowed to reopen in April. Yet this move did little to help the viability of movie theaters' reopening because he failed to account for the lack of new films that might draw viewers. Thus, even though theaters were allowed to reopen in April, in Athens, University 16 (located in Oconee, Kemp's home county) was the only theater that began this process in May before fully reopening in August. During the spring and most of the summer, Hollywood delayed the release of its major tentpoles, leaving reopened theaters with many offerings that resembled the library content streamers were licensing to create the appearance of catalogue depth. The major film studios assembled lists of a variety of digital cinema package (DCP) offerings based on different franchises (such as *Lord of the Rings*), periods ("Return to the '80s"), subsidiary companies ("DreamWorks Animation Classics"), genres ("Comedies"), auteurs ("Hitchcock"), and of course some more curious groupings such as the offering of films made by Johns, as in "John Carpenter/John Hughes." The size of these combo drives varied, and theaters were under no obligation to book all the titles on a drive, but fees went down if a theater booked repeatedly from a single drive. These studio drives help account for why theatrical reopenings leaned heavily into older titles. For their inaugural week of reopening, the University 16 offered an array of library titles from the past several years, ranging from *Aquaman* to *A Madea Family Funeral*. *Trolls World Tour* was the only new film on offer.

In addition to the limited availability of films to screen, theaters also had to find ways to comply with large-gathering restrictions and to implement social-distancing measures. In the first stage of reopening in the Athens area, University 16 started with limited-capacity private bookings. For a hundred dollars patrons could book a private screening for ten people. Rather than restricting seating in the theater, this solution allowed patrons to attend a movie with other friends or family members in their "bubble" or "pod." In theory, this reopening strategy, which gave people control over where they could sit in the theater, offered audiences the most say over their theatrical experience and exposure level. However, this was a significantly limited reopening in terms of both options and capacity.

Across the United States, state reopening policies and procedures were inconsistent, and in some cases corporations and professional organizations filled in policy gaps with business-specific protocols. NATO launched CinemaSafe, a program with facility and hygiene standards that supplemented state regulations, to help theaters establish benchmarks for reopening.[23] Other than enhanced cleaning procedures and new hand-sanitizer stations, these guidelines did not require theaters to outlay significant costs to improve facilities, such as HVAC upgrades. The guidelines do, however, outline a number of different expectations for their minimum-wage workers and patrons, such as appropriate social distancing, mask wearing, and handwashing that rely on individual compliance from workers and patrons. After meeting these benchmarks, University 16 was allowed to fully reopen on August 21 with new films such as *Unhinged* on screens, which opened nationally to $601,032 USD. Despite these attempts at new safety measures, box-office numbers demonstrated that audiences were not returning to theaters in significant numbers. Corporate policies maintained national standards, but regional politics played an important role in reopening. University 16 and Beechwood are both part of the same theater chain and are located within five miles of each other, but the mere fact that they operate in different counties created different timelines for reopening.

CINÉ

Ciné, in Clarke County, has been operated in Athens as a nonprofit arthouse movie theater (under the name Athens Film Art Institute [AFAI]) since 2009. As the only independent arthouse movie theater in the area, and the only movie theater downtown, it holds a unique cultural position for Athenians. Ciné is mission-driven and aspires to "inspire, educate and build community through art and culture" while also serving all members of the community.[24] In order to meet its mission, the theater does more than screen arthouse fare: it also hosts events, often with University of Georgia partnerships; provides a space for community organization; and, as a theater located downtown and within walking distance of college housing, it also shows Hollywood tentpoles to attract a broader audience. As a business it differs from the local GTC chain in two fundamental ways: first, decisions about business affairs are determined by a board of directors comprised of members of the community, such as myself, in conjunction with an executive director; second, Ciné owns its building and rents the adjacent space to a popular local restaurant. As a mission-driven theater with cultural cachet and nonprofit status (which gives the organization the opportunity to apply for grants and allows for

The Georgia Theater Company's Beechwood Cinemas in Athens remained closed longer than University 16. Even after the complex reopened, its signage announced its struggles. Author photo.

fundraising), Ciné's response to the pandemic looked different than that of other theaters in Athens.

Amid the shutdown, independent film distribution company Kino Lorber quickly set up a system to distribute new films and to support shuttered theaters. Launching KinoNow in 2019 as an "arthouse iTunes," Kino Lorber took advantage of an existing streaming platform, which added a new feature during the pandemic called Kino Marquee. The service was launched in 2019 with Cannes Grand Jury Prize winner *Bacurau* and *Sorry We Missed You*. Using Kino Marquee, audience members could rent a new movie for $12. Participating theaters, such as Ciné, received 50 percent of the rental fee.[25] In May, Kino Lorber released its total streaming box-office numbers through April 30 to *IndieWire*. *Bacurau* was the top Kino Marquee performer, bringing in $100,152 on the virtual platform, but these numbers were skewed by the fact that approximately ten theaters accounted for 40 percent of the gross. In contrast to other VOD releases, which were seen as a threat to theaters, those released through Kino Marquee explicitly supported independent and arthouse theaters. Box-office revenue through Kino Marquee was one of the few options for arthouse theaters, even though the amounts were nominal. With minimal income and no clear end to the pandemic in sight, many independent and arthouse theaters came up with nonscreening strategies to help theaters stay afloat.

Ciné developed several solutions that helped the theater stay visible in the community and continue to operate even while the doors remained closed. Like many small businesses, Ciné qualified for stimulus programs, such as the Payroll Protection Program (PPP) loans, as well as other state and local grants. Ciné also received donations and encouraged patrons to buy and renew memberships and seats in the theater in the effort to help keep it afloat. However, by April, Ciné's executive director, Pamela Kohn, and the board had to look for other potential revenue options while the theater remained closed. While we considered safe ways to reopen amid both the July peak and, in Athens, the more significant August–September peak that coincided with college students returning to campus, Ciné sold various branded apparel and "Movie Night To-Go" kits with popcorn and concessions. Both of these strategies provided more tangible connections to the theater and the theatergoing experience than donations.

Athens provides a microcosm of theatrical reopenings and pandemic business practices. The GTC relied on private bookings and partial reopening, whereas Ciné was supported throughout the spring and summer through an array of funding sources, ranging from virtual screenings to retail offerings to grants and donations. The differences between the reopening plans not only reflect what was available to businesses of different sizes, but they also highlight the impact of political differences on reopening policies. Lack of federal support to shuttered movie theaters and repeated policy failures, both state and national, that allowed the virus to spread continuously throughout 2020 necessitated different scales of response, whether that came from industry leaders like NATO, community leaders, individual businesses, or private donors. Theaters around the US had to rethink their business practices and, as a result, had to consider how to transform key aspects of the theatrical experience for the pandemic climate.

THE "THEATRICAL EXPERIENCE" DURING THE PANDEMIC

In a May 7 *Variety* article, Brent Lang and Rebecca Rubin claimed, "*Tenet* is more than a movie. It's the spark that cinemas are counting on to ignite a movie going revival in the U.S. and beyond."[26] From the first time *Tenet* was bumped until the final decision to release the film theatrically, this sentiment—that *Tenet* would bring the film industry out of the pandemic darkness to bask in the glow of the movie screen—was commonly espoused in the trades, popular press, and by director Christopher Nolan himself. Nolan, who has been a vocal supporter of 35mm film in a digital world, was an ideal advocate for the importance of theatrical distribution. He penned an op-ed in the *Washington Post* in March lobbying for theaters to receive government assistance and stressing the importance of the social experience of theatrical filmgoing and the healing potential of theatrical spaces in the postpandemic world.

Moviegoing was transformed during the pandemic. People did

not return to the theater in the way Nolan imagined, but the pandemic did not eradicate the desire for social viewing. Some theaters around the world reopened, but beyond China, there was no major global return to the movies. Some people went to see movies in theaters; others stayed home and tried to find alternate ways to watch movies with friends and family. In the United States theatrical experiences varied greatly by region and depended on whether indoor theaters were open for business or if drive-in theaters were an option. Many people sought out different ways to mimic social aspects of the theatrical experience.

Social viewing platforms are not pandemic innovations. The video game live-streaming platform Twitch, which launched in 2011, includes channels where people can watch movie and television shows together. Although these streams sometimes violate copyright laws, they exemplify that Twitch, as T. L. Taylor explains, "has offered players of all kinds an opportunity to build audiences interested in observing, commenting, and playing alongside them."[27] In this sense, these channels provided a precursor for some of the social viewing services and Chrome browser extensions that became popular in 2020.

Interactive browser extensions for film and television discovered new life amid shelter in place. Scener, introduced in 2018, was modeled after Twitch but with a focus specific to film and television. Scener was envisioned as a platform to allow directors and actors to comment in conjunction with streamed content or to let comedians perform screening-based live comedy (akin to RiffTrax). The platform offers users several options for choosing real-time commentary, including participating in live audio/video or text chat-streams that run alongside a window featuring a film or television show. During the pandemic, services like Scener reimagined the viewing experience for families and friends who wanted to watch movies and shows together. Scener CEO Joe Braidwood explained that the service has grown exponentially to half a million active users per week in 2020, although it is significantly less popular than Twitch, with its fifteen million daily users.[28]

Over the spring and summer of 2020, many streaming services developed their own platform-specific services, such as Amazon Watch Party and Hulu Watch Party, but some social streaming apps work across multiple streamers. Teleparty (formerly known as Netflix Party) works across multiple platforms and, with over ten million downloads worldwide, claims to be the most downloaded social TV app. These services offer similar features, inviting users to log in to their streaming service and invite friends to join a "watch party" or "screening room." All participants must be registered users of the streaming service in order to access the film, which is how these services protect themselves from copyright violations. Since viewers are not in the room together, in order to make the viewing a social "event," the social streaming apps seem to rely on viewers to comment more than they might in a theater or even as a group watching a movie at home.

Apps and extensions are effective at facilitating social viewing, but it is very different than the social experience of theatergoing. Movie theaters offer a more immersive experience and create conditions that induce audiences to focus on the screen while being aware of the jumps, screams, nervous-energy laughter, and tears of those around them in the theater. Most apps (with the exception of Scener) cannot show you the physical responses of your friends and family. Other drawbacks are that these extensions only work if you are streaming on your computer, and the chat feature makes it impossible to watch in full-screen mode, both of which make these apps an inadequate replacement for those who miss the immersive big-screen experience.

For those looking for a big-screen experience and the ability to distance safely from other patrons, drive-ins offered one of the best moviegoing options in 2020. Starting as early as March, drive-ins experienced a significant revival during the pandemic; the 305 remaining drive-ins across the United States accounted for the primary source of theatrical revenue over the summer.[29] The independent horror film *The Wretched* was even able to surpass the $1 million box-office mark in June just by playing drive-ins.[30] In general the ambient light pollution and the reliance on FM stations for sound are not considered conducive to creating ideal screening environments for theatrical releases, which are lit, color-timed, and mixed for an indoor theatrical experience.

Prior to 2020, the Vineland Drive-In, located in City of Industry, California, was a great place for inexpensive double features (and triple features of new movies on weekends). But it sits adjacent to a busy railroad that interrupts screenings with whistles and bright lights. Despite these limitations to the theatrical environment, Vineland played host to theatrical film premieres such as Dave Franco's directorial debut, *The Return*. Franco commented on the image and sound, saying that "certain scenes are darker than we intended when they aren't that dark on normal movie theater screens and there's certain sounds that aren't as accentuated because they're coming through the FM radio."[31] While few directors envision their premieres at a drive-in, this kind of outdoor event provided the closest thing to a theatrical premiere during the pandemic.

During the summer, as select new movies saw theatrical releases, some consumers felt comfortable enough to return to theaters. As the number of open theaters increased, Warner Bros. considered how to release the long-delayed *Tenet*. In contrast with Disney's initial decision about *Mulan*, Warner Bros. decided to give *Tenet* the exclusive theatrical release that Christopher Nolan wanted and had promised audiences throughout the summer. At the time of *Tenet*'s release over Labor Day weekend, 65 percent of the world's theaters were open, but key markets such as Los Angeles and New York remained closed. Although many people were unable or unwilling to return to theaters, industry discourse focused on excitement over the film's release. When the film was released, the popular press reported on a tweet from Tom Cruise that featured a video of his journey to mask up and watch *Tenet* in a London theater. In this video, the big-screen action star turns to the camera and declares, "Great to be back in the theater with everyone!"[32] *Variety* chose to report on Nolan fans booking flights to states with open theaters where they could watch the film.[33] Despite the enthusiasm and anticipation reported in the press, the film's box-office totals of $20 million USD over the Labor Day holiday failed to fulfill Nolan's dream that this film would restore moviegoing to its prepandemic popularity and indicated to the industry that September was still too early to reopen movie theaters.

Over the course of the pandemic there were many industry-sanctioned ways to watch movies communally, but individuals also found their own ways to share films together. During the spring and summer I watched countless movies with friends by syncing up our start time and texting or periodically chatting over Zoom. While many of these movie dates with friends have been ad hoc, my husband and I have a standing movie date with three couples in California that has been running since April 4 without a break. We both miss going to the movies, but this weekly gathering with friends across the country has strengthened personal relationships and been invaluable to our social well-being during the pandemic. It is also a way to watch movies and keep in touch with friends that would have never occurred to us without the pandemic. Whether these pandemic-specific solutions will remain in our lives when we are ready to return to theaters en masse remains to be seen.

EXHIBITION: LOOKING FORWARD

Film exhibitions, much like concerts and live sporting events, are in-person experiences that are important pieces of regional economies and the global media industries. With the exception of nationwide event businesses such as LiveNation or Ticketmaster, which had little to do during the pandemic, local economies involved in exhibition suffered the most: the temporarily shuttered movie theaters, indie clubs, and the bars and restaurants surrounding stadiums. Meanwhile, film studios found ways to distribute their films and recuperate some costs, and sports seasons resumed and fulfilled their media contracts. Many exhibition businesses also struggled because responses to the pandemic differed by region and nation; some countries kept theaters closed while others reopened them, leaving small theaters scrambling to find ways to generate income even with reduced audiences. Although many theaters were only empowered to respond to the present effects of the pandemic, powerful chains like AMC were already thinking about the postpandemic future and the deleterious effects of new films being distributed directly to one of the many streaming platforms.

The effect of the pandemic on event venues has been uneven (much like the official responses), but ultimately, for movie theaters, the pandemic simply sped up inevitable changes. Many movie theaters and music venues closed permanently during 2020, and it is likely that many more businesses will shutter before the end of the pandemic without continued federal intervention such as the Shut-tered Venue Operators Grant, which was signed into law at the end of December. Although music venues have been hard-hit, movie the-aters, especially chains like AMC, have been more effective at sur-viving the shutdowns and reduced audiences. Teetering on the edge of bankruptcy and with limited reopening prospects in the spring, AMC was still better positioned than many event venues around the country.

Certain aspects of film exhibition — such as the low cost of putting a film on the screen (relative to booking a band) and the fact that movie watching is a stationary activity that makes it easier to socially distance — made movie theaters easier to open. But most notably, the-aters also had support from the film industry, which offered lower-cost library content for phased reopening and a willingness to come to the bargaining table to develop future plans to ensure that exhibi-tion and streaming can coexist postpandemic. Exhibition practices have changed, but many of these are more a result of changes to the distribution landscape rather than the pandemic.

It is unclear when US theater attendance will pick up again. The Chinese box office surpassed North America for the first time ever in October 2020 and continued to thrive at the end of the year. In the US the prognosis throughout 2020 continued to be grim, even as select films were released at the end of the summer and some studios started to release selected box-office numbers again. *Tenet*'s paltry $20 million opening weekend sparked debate between industry ana-lysts and journalists about whether the theatrical release could be counted a success within the context of the pandemic. While some declared the film a flop, others felt this was a "positive indicator of de-mand."[34] Speculation about the future of theatrical exhibition ranges from cautiously optimistic to completely panicked, but regardless of where one falls on the spectrum, during 2020 those tracking theatri-cal releases had to rethink their definitions of box-office success.

In terms of Hollywood's business practices, one of the most sig-nificant consequences of the pandemic disruptions could be tied to how financial data is reported. The pandemic paused the industry practice of daily box-office reporting, and new release strategies from studios facing narrower profit margins might further muddle the reporting. Much to the frustration of creatives, the practice of withholding viewer data has been common at Netflix, but theatrical box-office information, much like Neilsen ratings, has always been accessible to executives as well as producers and talent who are monitoring the success of their projects. Digital and hybrid releases allow studios to obfuscate box-office numbers and frame them in a positive light. It often can be hard to change longstanding practices, but disruptions such as those caused by the pandemic can and likely will be used as an excuse to make changes favorable to studios rather than exhibitors.

WHERE DO WE GO FROM HERE?

HOLLYWOOD SHUTDOWN COVERS the first nine months of the pandemic, a period marked by increased attention to on-set health and production safety and experimental distribution and exhibition strategies. Meanwhile the industry waited and hoped for a return to "business as usual." This period can be divided into two distinct stages: the spring, which was characterized by widespread global shutdowns; and summer, which featured haphazard and makeshift reopenings. Around the world countries experienced huge spikes in viral infections in March and April, but many nations gradually reopened during the summer (whether or not that was advisable). In China the film industry was shut down for a relatively short time. Filmmakers returned to set, and people started going to the movies again, helping the Chinese box-office totals surpass those in North America for the first time ever by the end of the year. However, even as countries created a new normal, scientists continued to warn that there would be a second wave of the virus in the winter.

In writing about democracy during this time of pandemic, legal scholars Miguel Poiares Maduro and Paul Kahn explain that "facts alone, even terrible facts, do not themselves determine 'what comes next.' . . . It may help to understand the scope of the crises of government."[1] As of this writing, the pandemic is ongoing, and, with no clear end in sight, it would be unadvisable to predict all the future effects of the COVID-19 pandemic on the media industries. However, it is not too soon to assess the scope of the crisis the coronavirus wrought. The events of the spring and summer of 2020 will undoubtedly impact the future of media in ways we cannot predict; however, the pandemic was not the only major event of 2020. As society reconciles many of the social and economic changes wrought by the pandemic, we will need to consider whether industrial shifts helped shape policy and antitrust decisions and social justice movements that were well underway prior to 2020.

The pandemic frequently occupied news cycles and changed how most people worked and spent their leisure time, but there were policy discussions and changes that happened separate from those related to the global crisis. Deregulation of the media industries paved the way for many of the changes we witnessed in 2020, but this does not have to be the direction of US policy. The major media regulation stories in 2020 seemed to be on opposite sides of the regulation spectrum: the tech antitrust hearings in July contrasted sharply with the repeal of the Paramount Decrees in August. Although deregulation of the media has historically received bipartisan support, the tech antitrust hearings in July might indicate new willingness to regulate tech companies. The hearings did not produce tangible outcomes, but the question will be how, or if, that affects entertainment media companies in the future. If the tech hearings reflected an interest in more regulation, the repeal of the Paramount Decrees was more consistent with the longer history of deregulation. From the perspective of lawmakers and regulators, Peter Labuza points out that the repeal of the Paramount Decrees reflects a broader Department of Justice "policy to review hundreds of legal orders that some refer to as 'horse and buggy' policies—ones so old that they no longer actually apply to the business they regulate."[2] The repeal now means that studios can resume some of their regional clearance practices, block bookings, and potentially buy up theaters (although the latter might be unappealing given the state of theatrical exhibition at the time of writing).

The Black Lives Matter movement and many of the specific calls for Hollywood to reckon with its whiteness have been part of recent national conversations about civil rights and representation since 2013 and 2015, respectively.[3] In 2020 the murders of George Floyd and Breonna Taylor set off a summer of worldwide protests against racial injustice and created a renewed sense of urgency to calls for justice. Prior to the pandemic, think tanks like the Annenberg Inclusion Initiative and UCLA's Bunche Center confronted problems in hiring pipelines, pay gaps, and other practices that perpetuate the white male dominance of Hollywood. The industry responded to concerns of white hegemony by greenlighting more projects featuring and about BIPOC characters, and the Academy announced new diversity and inclusion requirements for Best Picture nominations, but these changes have been criticized as superficial as long as Hollywood companies are still led predominantly by white men.[4] The protests inspired renewed reflection, but there is still a tremendous amount of work to be done to transform hiring and mentoring practices—all of which has been further complicated by the pandemic-related disruptions to workplace practices.

The economic and health crises also (hopefully temporarily) marginalized ongoing concerns about sexual harassment in the industry. In the wake of high-profile, documented accusations against powerful men—including Harvey Weinstein, former WB chairman and CEO Kevin Tsujihara, and former CBS chairman and CEO Les Moonves—groups like TimesUp and industry unions including SAG-AFTRA have endeavored to create better systems for reporting sexual harassment via hotlines and on set. Changes to create equity in hiring, eliminate harassment, and punish harassers were a work-in-progress when the pandemic hit. The ramifications of this pause in transforming the industry environment will linger as activists continue to advocate for change as Hollywood recovers.

The fall saw initial increases in positive COVID-19 cases as college students returned to campus. As experts predicted, the holiday season brought even more dire infection and casualty numbers. In response, Hollywood studios continued to delay major releases or alter their release strategies. Although the *Mulan* release was not a financial success, by the fall studios realized that streaming or VOD would be the only way to effectively release new films amid a pandemic with no end in sight. Several studios, including Universal and Paramount, have held back some titles for 2021 theatrical release, while WarnerMedia opted to put their entire 2021 slate, including tentpoles like *Wonder Woman 1984*, on HBOMax in order to boost the subscription numbers for the struggling service. As I finished this book in March 2021, three vaccines have been approved in the US, and despite early hiccups, the rollout improved tremendously after February. Optimism surrounding vaccinations and President Biden's promise that vaccines would be available to everyone in the United States by May 1 inspired some hope for a return to normal. Notably for the film industry, movie theaters finally reopened in Los Angeles and New York in March 2021. However, some studios have continued to proceed with caution. Unfortunately, vaccinations around the world have been slower than the US effort; the pandemic is still ongoing, and studios have continued to delay their summer release schedule for films like *Minions 2* and *F9*. Just as new developments shook the media industries during the fall and winter of 2020, new decisions in 2021 will complicate the legacy of COVID-19 and its impact on Hollywood.

The shattering of release windows will continue to impact how audiences watch films around the world. And, although it is a direct negotiation point between studio executives and theater owners, it will have an impact on media industry workers, from the extras to the stars and from the editors to the directors. Residuals (payments for the reuse of material in addition to backend payments for stars) are dependent on a film's release. A successful theatrical film can garner long-term success (and residual payments) when the film is shown on TV or licensed to the streaming services. Additionally, above-the-line talent, such as directors and stars, are often contractually guaranteed bonuses based on box-office performance. With many theatrical films headed directly to streaming in 2020 and 2021, there continues to be no clear resolution for how above-the-line creatives will be compensated.

It is also important to consider the long-term consequences of pandemic-related cancellations. Throughout 2020 productions were cancelled and new filmmakers were unable to show their finished work at festivals. The stoppages and slowdowns in production and distribution meant many internships were cancelled, denying the next generation of industry workers the chance to add essential experience to their resumes.[5] Some students were able to do virtual internships that meant they did not need to live in Los Angeles for the summer, thus lowering some of the expenses associated with interning. However, Hollywood places high value on industry experience, and with experiential learning cancelled or shifted online, this will add obstacles for students and media industry aspirants in a business that is already notoriously difficult to access. Amid the pandemic many employers adjusted expectations, but it is unclear whether that level of empathy and understanding will extend in the coming years.

Hollywood as an industry also needs to consider the possibility that we might experience another pandemic. We need to learn from our failures and work collaboratively to curb the spread rather than waiting to be saved by a vaccine. Although there was a hundred-year gap between the Spanish flu and COVID-19, numerous scientists and epidemiologists predict that continued damage to the environment will lead to more pandemics in our future.[6] Hollywood executives, after some trial and error, have found some solutions to continue to profit and will likely be more prepared if we find ourselves in another global health crisis. Talent, both above and below the line, will need to be particularly mindful in all future negotiations to make sure that they do not suffer long-term consequences of the studios' pandemic solutions.

ACKNOWLEDGMENTS

FIRST AND FOREMOST, thank you to all the essential workers who provide care labor and sustain the national infrastructure for those of us who were able to work from home throughout the pandemic. *Hollywood Shutdown* was written on a very abbreviated timeline, which would not have been possible without the efficiency of the University of Texas Press editorial team and the librarians at the University of Georgia who made many resources digitally available in 2020. Special thanks to Jim Burr, who has discussed the manuscript at each stage and helped usher me through this second project. As this project moved into production, I was also thrilled to continue working with Lynne Ferguson, who is efficient, easy to work with, and attentive to detail. Finally, thank you to my department head, James Hamilton, who helped me to secure indexer funds.

I am tremendously appreciative of my summer class. In summer 2020, I was supposed to take a group of students to Los Angeles for eight weeks. When the pandemic halted all travel plans, my summer "Media Industries in Context" class turned into a course on "Media Industries in the Pandemic." Designing this course and talking about the various changes to the industry was certainly part of the foundation for this project. Thank you to my EMST 4050 students—Shelby, Harrison, Meghan, Julia, Ana, Lili, Josh, Maddie, Hayden, Kyanna, Drew, and Margaret—for being so quick to adapt and engage in thoughtful conversations during a tumultuous historical moment. A very special thanks to Margaret for keeping me up to date on various Georgia-based productions over the summer and beyond. You are a resilient group, and I am confident that you are all prepared to handle any changes wrought by the pandemic.

Over the course of the year, virtual movie nights and Athens-pods have been the core of my social life. In April, our annual horror film fest became a weekly Zoom event and reshaped our weekends. George, Zoey, James, Lindsay, Claire, and David, I am appreciative of the fun themes and thoughtful film curation and look forward to an in-person movie marathon in the future. Thank you to Elizabeth

Affuso, Kristen Fuhs, Luke Pebler, and Suzanne Scott for lively debates over time-travel films and dedication to Gerard Butler's oeuvre. Thank you to Luci Marzola, my favorite collaborator and always generous editor. Alexa Bankert, James Biddle, Shira Chess, Matthew and Kat Evans, Anne Gilbert, Katy O'Brien, and Michael O'Neal, thank you for your friendship and support, via texts, Zooms, and backyard distanced hangouts. Finally, thank you to my moms, who moved to Athens only a year before the pandemic; I am grateful that despite the pandemic we managed to have weekly dinners in the backyard. Writing during the pandemic would have been impossible without the support of David Lerner. Our home was also enlivened by our always entertaining cat (Benson) and pandemic puppy (Gertie) who vied for space in my lap as I wrote this book. Although we have years of practice working from home and sharing a home office, nothing prepared us for our home to do extra duty as gym, movie theater, and site of many Zoom hangouts. I look forward to venturing out of the house, but you are the best quarantine companions I could ever imagine.

NOTES

INTRODUCTION. HOLLYWOOD RESPONDS TO A PANDEMIC

1. Jennifer Holt, "It's Not Film, It's TV: Rethinking Industrial Identity," *Jump Cut* 52, Summer 2010, http://ejumpcut.org/archive/jc52.2010/HoltNotFilm TV/index.html.

2. Political theorists have expanded on this discussion of precarity as a condition of capitalism; see Isabell Lorey, *State of Insecurity: Government of the Precarious*, trans. Aileen Derieg (New York: Verso, 2015); and Brett Neilson and Ned Rossiter, "Precarity as a Political Concept, or, Fordism as Exception," *Theory, Culture and Society* 25, nos. 7–8 (2008).

3. Bureau of Labor Statistics, "Economic News Release—Employment Situation News Release," US Bureau of Labor Statistics website, May 8, 2020, https:// www.bls.gov/news.release/archives/empsit_05082020.htm.

4. Neil Walker, "The Crisis of Democratic Leadership in Times of Pandemic," *Democracy in Times of Pandemic*, ed. Miguel Poiares and Paul Kahn (Cambridge: Cambridge University Press, 2020), 28.

5. Jennifer Holt, *Empires of Entertainment: Media Industries and the Politics of Deregulation, 1980–1996* (New Brunswick, NJ: Rutgers University Press, 2011).

6. The ecology and language of services, platforms, portals, and apps has gotten increasingly complex (and confusing). For a lucid discussion of this, see Ramon Lobato, *Netflix Nations: The Geography of Digital Distribution* (New York: NYU Press, 2019), 7–10.

CHAPTER 1. PRODUCTION

1. Patrick Frater, "China's Film and TV Production Makes Partial Restart after Coronavirus Hiatus," *Variety*, April 3, 2020, https://variety.com/2020/film /asia/coronavirus-china-film-tv-production-partial-restart-1234570137/.

2. Brent Lang, "Hollywood Studios Assembling Coronavirus Strategy Teams," *Variety*, February 28, 2020, https://variety.com/2020/film/news/holly wood-coronavirus-no-time-to-die-mulan-1203518001/.

3. Much of the discussion around the impact on distribution and exhibition in the first months centered around the fact that China's shutdowns coincided with the Chinese New Year. For further discussion of this impact, see chapter 3 in this book; Nancy Tartaglione, "Chinese New Year Films Cancellation Could Mean A $1B+ Loss for Global Box Office in 2020: What's the Impact on Hollywood?," *Deadline*, January 23, 2020, https://deadline.com/2020/01/chinese-new -year-films-cancellation-impact-global-hollywood-box-office-analysis-1202838

847/; Brent Lang and Rebecca Rubin, "What Happens If Coronavirus Causes US Theaters to Close?," *Variety*, March 4, 2020, https://variety.com/2020/film /news/coronavirus-movie-theater-closure-1203523653/; and Anthony D'Alessandro, "'Mulan' Eyes $80M–$90M+ Opening on Tracking in the Wake of Coronavirus Stateside Fears Ramping Up," *Deadline*, March 5, 2020, https://deadline .com/2020/03/mulan-opening-weekend-projections-1202875132/.

4. Nellie Andreeva, "TV Studios in Strike-Preparation Mode ahead of WGA Contract Negotiations with Overall Deals at Stake and Streamers as Wild Card," *Deadline*, November 27, 2019, https://deadline.com/2019/11/tv-studios -strike-preparation-mode-wga-contract-negotiations-netflix-streamers-overall -deals-1202795768/.

5. For more on the labor conditions that inspired network production of reality television, see Chad Raphael, "The Political Economic Origins of Reali-TV," *Reality TV—Remaking Television Culture*, 2nd ed., ed. Laurie Ouellette and Susan Murray (New York: NYU Press, 2009), 123–140.

6. For an in-depth look on the worker cultures that develop alongside these kinds of innovations, see Vicki Mayer, *Below the Line: Producers and Production Studies in the New Television Economy* (Durham, NC: Duke University Press, 2011).

7. Nellie Andreeva, "'The Young and the Restless' & 'The Bold and the Beautiful' Suspend Production amid Coronavirus Crisis," *Deadline*, March 16, 2020, https://deadline.com/2020/03/the-young-and-the-restless-the-bold-and-the -beautiful-suspend-production-coronavirus-crisis-1202885176/.

8. Throughout the summer analysts anticipated that insurance companies might face a number of lawsuits. In theory, this area could become a rich resource for those examining the impact of the pandemic on Hollywood. Select resources on the challenges for insurers and studios during the developing crisis include: Anousha Sakoui and Ryan Faughnder, "Hollywood Faces Huge Losses from Coronavirus: Can the Insurance Industry Bail It Out?," *Los Angeles Times*, March 27, 2020, https://www.latimes.com/entertainment-arts/business/story /2020-03-27/hollywood-is-shut-down-and-facing-losses-can-the-insurance -industry-bail-it-out; Chris Lindahl, "Coronavirus Production Insurance? No Such Thing: Here's How Hollywood Will Cope," *IndieWire*, April 20, 2020, https:// www.indiewire.com/2020/04/coronavirus-delays-production-insurance -hollywood-1202225664/; Jill Goldsmith, "Reopening Hollywood: Two Firms Take First Steps toward COVID-19 Insurance for Indie Industry Desperate to Yell 'Action!,'" *Deadline*, September 9, 2020, https://deadline.com/2020/09/covid -insurance-indie-film-tv-producers-production-restart-repoening-hollywood -1234572564/; Ashley Cullins, "Ben Affleck Starrer 'Hypnotic' Sparks COVID-Related Insurance Suit," *Hollywood Reporter*, September 9, 2020, https://www .hollywoodreporter.com/thr-esq/ben-affleck-starrer-hypnotic-sparks-covid -related-insurance-suit; and Stephan Kahl, "Hollywood's Insurer Braces for Claims

Due to COVID-Related Movie, TV Shutdowns," *Insurance Journal*, October 6, 2020, https://www.insurancejournal.com/news/national/2020/10/06/585495.htm.

9. Chris Gardner, "Entertainment Industry Has Lost 'Many' of Its 890,000 Jobs during COVID-19 Pandemic, L.A. Official Says," *Hollywood Reporter*, May 20, 2020, https://www.hollywoodreporter.com/news/entertainment-industry-has -lost-890000-jobs-covid-19-pandemic-la-official-says-1295373.

10. For more on the pandemic's impact on actors, see Kate Fortmueller, *Below the Stars: How the Labor of Extras and Actors Shapes Media Production* (Austin: University of Texas Press, 2021), 159–164.

11. Kim Masters, "Coronavirus and Hollywood: How Are Industry Workers Faring?," *The Business*, March 30, 2020, https://www.kcrw.com/culture/shows /the-business/jobless-hollywood-workers-cope-with-coronavirus/coronavirus -hollywood-industry-workers-coping.

12. Matt Grobar, "Post-Production Industry Fears Work Will Dry Up during Shutdown, Ponders a Remote Editing Future," *Deadline*, March 23, 2020, https:// deadline.com/2020/03/hollywood-post-production-coronvirus-editors-work -from-home-future-1202886816/.

13. Nellie Andreeva and Dominic Patten, "Animation Production Is Still Going, Sometimes Slower, Amid Coronavirus Crisis," *Deadline*, March 24, 2020, https://deadline.com/2020/03/animation-tv-series-continue-coronavirus-challen ges-1202890786/.

14. Fortmueller, *Below the Stars*, 137–149.

15. David Robb, "Bob's Burgers Animation House Bento Box Hiring 20 Freelancers in Production amid Hollywood Shutdown," *Deadline*, March 25, 2020, https://deadline.com/2020/03/bento-box-animation-hiring-coronvirus-bobs -burgers-1202891292/.

16. For the full call, see "Netflix Q1 2020 Earnings Call," April 21, 2020, https://www.youtube.com/watch?v=d-s50JhC4aw.

17. Nellie Andreeva, "Reopening Hollywood: How Gloria Calderón Kellett Led 'Real & Honest' Conversation with Ideas Ranging from Quick Tests & Drama Camps to Sexy Salutes," *Deadline*, April 21, 2020, https://deadline.com /2020/04/reopening-hollywood-tv-production-ideas-coronavirus-return-gloria -calderon-kellett-1202912451/.

18. Reid Nakamura, "How 'One Day at a Time' Pulled Off an Animated Episode—With Lin-Manuel Miranda!—In only 8 Weeks," *The Wrap*, June 16, 2020, https://www.thewrap.com/how-one-day-at-a-time-pulled-off-an-animated -episode-with-lin-manuel-miranda-in-only-8-weeks/.

19. Michael Tueth, "Back to the Drawing Board: The Family in Animated Television Comedy," in *Prime Time Animation: Television Animation and American Culture*, ed. Carol Stabile and Mark Harrison (Taylor & Francis, 2003), 135.

20. Nakamura, "How 'One Day at a Time' Pulled Off an Animated Episode."

21. Daniel Holloway, "How Trevor Noah Brought 'The Daily Show' into His

Home—And the Future," *Variety*, August 25, 2020, https://variety.com/2020/tv /features/trevor-noah-daily-show-home-coronavirus-1234746711/.

22. For more on the 2020 ratings picture, see Rick Porter, "The Grim TV Ratings Reality of 2020," *Hollywood Reporter*, December 23, 2020, https://www .hollywoodreporter.com/live-feed/the-grim-tv-ratings-reality-of-2020.

23. Amanda Hess, "'The Credibility Bookcase' Is the Quarantine's Hottest Accessory," *New York Times*, May 1, 2020, https://www.nytimes.com/2020/05/01 /arts/quarantine-bookcase-coronavirus.html.

24. This detail has been widely reported and confirmed, but Noah does not discuss the details publicly. See Holloway, "How Trevor Noah Brought 'The Daily Show' into His Home."

25. Bernard Timberg and Bob Erler, *Television Talk: A History of the TV Talk Show* (Austin: University of Texas Press, 2002), 14.

26. Daniel Steinhart, *Runaway Hollywood: Internationalizing Postwar Production and Location Shooting* (Berkeley: University of California Press, 2019), 26.

27. Nancy Tartaglione, "Reopening Hollywood: How Baltasar Kormakur Re-Started Production on Netflix's 'Katla' amid COVID-19 Lockdown in Iceland," *Deadline*, May 1, 2020, https://deadline.com/2020/05/baltasar-kormakur -interview-resumes-production-katla-netflix-iceland-coronavirus-1202923259/.

28. Elaine Lowe, "Inside Netflix's Quest to Become a Global TV Giant," *Variety*, July 30, 2020, https://variety.com/2020/tv/news/netflix-global-tv-pro duction-bela-bajaria-1234720101/.

29. "State of Georgia Film & Television Production Best Practices to Reduce the Spread of COVID-19," May 22, 2020, https://www.georgia.org/sites/default /files/2020-05/covid-19_georgia_film.tv_best_practices.pdf.

30. "State of Georgia Film & Television Production Best Practices."

31. Brett, April 21, 2020, 12:34am, https://twitter.com/relentlessbored/status /1252818020776333312?lang=en.

32. Andreas Wiseman, "Universal's 'Jurassic World: Dominion' on Course to be First Major Studio Movie Back Underway in UK, Detailed Protocols Revealed," *Deadline*, June 15, 2020, https://deadline.com/2020/06/universal-juras sic-world-production-uk-chris-pratt-bryce-dallas-howard-1202958819/.

33. Bryn Elise Sandberg, "Tyler Perry Talks 'Camp Quarantine' and Challenges of Filming amid a Pandemic," *Hollywood Reporter*, July 29, 2020, https:// www.hollywoodreporter.com/news/tyler-perry-talks-camp-quarantine-challen ges-filming-a-pandemic-1304909.

34. Derek Thompson, "Hygiene Theater Is a Huge Waste of Time," *The Atlantic*, July 27, 2020, https://www.theatlantic.com/ideas/archive/2020/07/scourge -hygiene-theater/614599/.

35. Kate Aurthur, "New Document Lays Out Plan to Resume Movie and TV Productions with Strict Quarantine Pods (Exclusive)," *Variety*, April 24, 2020, https://variety.com/2020/biz/news/production-plan-coronavirus-1234589286/.

36. Cynthia Littleton and Kate Aurthur, "Industry Infighting, Union Turf

Battles Slow Development of Back-to-Work Plan," *Variety*, May 21, 2020, https://variety.com/2020/film/news/production-guidelines-white-paper-amptp-iatse-1234613975/.

37. "Industry-Wide Labor Management Safety Committee Task Force, Proposed Health and Safety Guidelines for Motion Picture, Television, and Streaming Productions During the COVID-19 Pandemic," June 1, 2020, 7.

38. DGA, SAG-AFTRA, IATSE, and Teamsters' Committees for COVID-19 Safety Guidelines, "The Safe Way Forward," released June 12, 2020.

39. Adam Epstein, "The Pandemic Has Turned Everyone into Gamers," *Quartz*, September 16, 2020, https://qz.com/1904276/everyone-is-playing-video-games-during-the-pandemic/; Noah Smith, "The Giants of the Video Game Industry Have Thrived in the Pandemic: Can the Success Continue?," *Washington Post*, May 12, 2020, https://www.washingtonpost.com/video-games/2020/05/12/video-game-industry-coronavirus/.

40. Bill Desowitz, "'The Mandalorian' Leads the Way: Real-Time Virtual Production Is Saving Hollywood during the Lockdown," *IndieWire*, May 8, 2020, https://www.indiewire.com/2020/05/the-mandalorian-real-time-virtual-production-saving-hollywood-lockdown-vfx-1202230120/.

CHAPTER 2. DISTRIBUTION

1. Alisa Perren, "Rethinking Distribution for the Future of Media Industry Studies," *Cinema Journal* 53, no. 2 (Spring 2013), 166.

2. For greater depth on the industrial history of cord-cutting and "cord nevers," see Amanda Lotz, *We Now Disrupt this Broadcast* (Cambridge, MA: MIT Press, 2018), 135–138.

3. Gavin Bridge, "Why Q2 Cord-Cutting Wasn't as Bad as Feared (But Not Good, Either)," *Variety*, August 7, 2020, https://variety.com/vip/why-q2-cord-cutting-wasnt-as-bad-as-feared-but-not-good-either-1234729182/.

4. Dade Hayes, "Streaming Subscribers Have Itchy Trigger Fingers during COVID-19, with Churn Rate Rising to 41%," *Deadline*, June 29, 2020, https://deadline.com/2020/06/streaming-subscribers-have-itchy-trigger-fingers-during-covid-19-with-churn-rate-rising-to-41-report-1202972533/.

5. For more on the history of film libraries, see Eric Hoyt, *Hollywood Vault: Film Libraries before Home Video* (Berkeley: University of California Press, 2014).

6. Michael Smith and Rahul Telang, *Streaming, Sharing, Stealing: Big Data and the Future of Entertainment* (Cambridge, MA: MIT Press, 2016), 64.

7. Amanda Lotz, "Q26: How Does Focusing on the US 'Streaming Wars' Mistake a Battle for the War?," *Netflix 30 Q&A*, August 31, 2020, http://www.amandalotz.com/netflix-30-qa/2020/8/31/q26-how-does-focusing-on-the-us-streaming-wars-mistake-a-battle-for-the-war.

8. For more on localized satellite content, see Jean Chalaby, *The Format Age* (Malden, MA: Polity Press, 2016); Joseph D. Straubhaar and Luiz G. Duarte,

"Adapting US Transnational Television Channels to a Complex World: From Cultural Imperialism to Localization to Hybridization," in *Transnational Television Worldwide: Towards a New Media Order* (London: I. B. Tauris, 2005). For more on localized streaming content, see Lobato, *Netflix Nations*.

9. For more on the licensing and distribution deals, see Tom Grater, "Netflix to Stream Classic Truffaut, Chaplin Pics in France after Library Deal with Mk2," *Deadline*, April 20, 2020, https://deadline.com/2020/04/netflix-mk2-stream -classic-truffaut-chaplin-pics-1202912478/; and Fabien Lemercier, "Netflix Continues to Splash the Cash on French Films," *Cineuropa*, October 7, 2020, https:// cineuropa.org/en/newsdetail/393435/.

10. Karen Petruska, "Content That Travels: International Content and Original Programming on U.S. Streaming Sites," *Flow*, April 22, 2015, https://www.flow journal.org/2015/04/content-that-travels-international/.

11. Jaap Verheul, "Opening the Vault: Streaming the Film Library in the Age of Pandemic Content," *Pandemic Media*, https://pandemicmedia.meson .press/chapters/time-temporality/opening-the-vault-streaming-the-film-library -in-the-age-of-pandemic-content/.

12. Todd Spangler and Brent Lang, "Why 'Harry Potter,' Other Big Movies Have Become Hot Commodities during COVID Pandemic," *Variety*, August 18, 2020, https://variety.com/2020/digital/news/harry-potter-movies-hbo-max-pea cock-covid-1234738031/.

13. Meg James, "HBO App Confusion Prompts WarnerMedia to Cancel HBO Now, HBO Go," *Los Angeles Times*, June 12, 2020, https://www.latimes .com/entertainment-arts/business/story/2020-06-12/hbo-go-hbo-now-canceled -warnermedia-hbo-max-launch.

14. Andrew Barker, "Judd Apatow on the Importance of Film Festivals Like SXSW," *Variety*, March 19, 2020, https://variety.com/2020/film/spotlight/judd -apatow-pete-davidson-sxsw-king-of-staten-island-1203538183/.

15. Dina Iordanova, "The Film Festival as an Industry Node," *Media Industries* 1, no. 3 (2015), https://doi.org/10.3998/mij.15031809.0001.302.

16. Tatiana Siegel, "Was Sundance a 'First Petri Dish' of Coronavirus in the States?," *Hollywood Reporter*, May 6, 2020, https://www.hollywoodreporter .com/features/was-sundance-a-first-petri-dish-coronavirus-states-1293378.

17. For more on the regional economy supported by SXSW, see Dan Solomon, "SXSW 2015: Meet Some Faces of the SXSW Economy," *Texas Monthly*, March 18, 2015, https://www.texasmonthly.com/the-daily-post/sxsw-2015-meet-some -faces-of-the-sxsw-economy/; and "Analysis of the Economic Benefit to the City of Austin from SXSW 2019," November 18, 2019, https://explore.sxsw.com /hubfs/2019%20SXSW%20Economic%20Impact%20Analysis%20-%20 11.18.19%20OPT.pdf.

18. Brent Lang, "Devastated Filmmakers Scrambling after SXSW Cancellation," *Variety*, March 10, 2020, https://variety.com/2020/film/news/sxsw-cancel lation-filmmakers-coronavirus-1203529235/.

19. Kaleem Aftab, "Should Filmmakers Accept Online Festival Premieres?" *Variety*, April 9, 2020, https://variety.com/2020/film/festivals/filmmakers-accept-online-festival-premieres-coronavirus-tribeca-cphdox-alex-winter-zappa-1234576233/.

20. For more on the debates between Netflix and Cannes, see Eric Kohn, "Netflix's Battle with Cannes: Why This Film Industry Showdown Can't Find a Solution," *IndieWire*, March 5, 2019, https://www.indiewire.com/2019/03/netflix-cannes-2019-competition-ban-1202048570/; Alissa Wilkinson, "Netflix v. Cannes: Why They're Fighting, What It Means for Cinema, and Who Really Loses?," *Vox*, April 13, 2018, https://www.vox.com/culture/2018/4/13/17229476/netflix-versus-cannes-ted-sarandos-thierry-fremaux-okja-meyerowitz-orson-welles-streaming-theater.

21. Elsa Keslassy, "Cannes Film Festival Won't Go Virtual If All Else Fails," *Variety*, April 7, 2020, https://variety.com/2020/film/global/cannes-film-festival-wont-go-virtual-coronavirus-1234572974/.

22. Kyle Buchanan, Manohla Dargis, and A. O. Scott, "What Do We Lose When Cannes Is Canceled?," *New York Times*, May 22, 2020, https://www.nytimes.com/2020/05/12/movies/cannes-critics.html.

23. Roger Smith, "DECANNESTRUCTION: What Is the Cannes Market and Does It Matter?," *Film Comment* 37, no. 4 (July/August 2001), 20.

24. For more on the history of the Marché du Film, see Marijke de Valck, *Film Festivals: From European Geopolitics to Global Cinephilia* (Amsterdam: Amsterdam University Press, 2007).

25. For trade reporting on the emergence of the dual markets, see Andreas Wiseman, "The Story Behind the Cannes Virtual Market(s): How Coronavirus Has Led to a New Way of Doing Business and an Unprecedented Agency Coalition," *Deadline*, May 26, 2020, https://deadline.com/2020/05/cannes-virtual-market-story-behind-coronavirus-new-way-doing-business-unprecedented-agency-coalition-1202939294/.

26. "The Marché Reveals Numbers as It Wraps Up Its First Ever Online Edition," Marché du Film, July 2, 2020, https://www.marchedufilm.com/news/the-marche-reveals-numbers-as-it-wraps-up-its-first-ever-online-edition/.

27. Charles Acland, *Screen Traffic: Movies, Multiplexes, and Global Culture* (Durham, NC: Duke University Press, 2003), 197–201.

28. Marissa Marr, "Redirecting Disney," *Wall Street Journal*, December 5, 2005, https://www.wsj.com/articles/SB113374725252213739.

29. Diane Garrett, "Theatrical Windows Shrink in 2006," *Variety*, March 12, 2007, https://variety.com/2007/digital/features/theatrical-windows-shrink-in-2006-1117961046/.

30. Pat Saperstein, "'Margin Call' Changes VOD Picture," *Variety*, December 18, 2011, https://variety.com/2011/film/news/margin-call-changes-vod-picture-1118047677/.

31. Tom Bruggemann and Anne Thompson, "Harvey Weinstein Explains

How 'Snowpiercer' Became a Gamechanger, We Crunch Theater vs. VOD Numbers," *IndieWire*, July 21, 2014, https://www.indiewire.com/2014/07/exclusive
-harvey-weinstein-explains-how-snowpiercer-became-a-gamechanger-we-crunch
-theater-vs-vod-numbers-191454/.

32. Susan Waxman, "Tension High at CinemaCon—NATO Explodes over Premium VOD," *The Wrap*, March 31, 2011, https://www.thewrap.com/tension
-high-cinemacon-between-studios-and-stressed-exhibitors-26014/; and Pamela McClintock, "Universal to Offer 'Tower Heist' on Early VOD for $59.99," October 5, 2011, https://www.hollywoodreporter.com/news/universal-tower-heist
-eddie-murphy-244601.

33. Jen Yamato, "Sony Responds to President Obama's Criticism: 'We Had No Choice, Still Hope to Release *The Interview*,'" *Deadline*, December 19, 2014, https://deadline.com/2014/12/sony-president-obama-the-interview-response
-1201330799/.

34. For more on *The Interview* and SPE's decision-making, see J. D. Connor, "The Sony Hack: Data and Decision in the Contemporary Studio," *Media Industries* 2, no. 2 (2015), https://quod.lib.umich.edu/m/mij/15031809.0002.203/—
sony-hack-data-and-decision-in-the-contemporary-studio?rgn=main;view=full
text;q1=connor.

35. Ultimately Paramount would decide to push its films to 2021, while Warner Bros. and Disney would release their tentpoles in 2020.

36. Anthony D'Alessandro, "'Trolls World Tour' Universal PVOD Racks Up Near Estimated $100M to Date," *Deadline*, April 28, 2020, https://deadline.com
/2020/04/trolls-world-tour-vod-revenue-universal-coronavirus-1202919723/.

37. Kim Masters, "NBCU's 'Trolls' Play: Stars Want Pay, But Will Studios Make Any Money?," *Hollywood Reporter*, May 6, 2020, https://www.hollywood
reporter.com/news/trolls-world-tour-stars-want-pay-but-will-studio-make-any
-money-1293394.

38. Rebecca Ford, "Inside Disney's Bold $200M Gamble on 'Mulan': 'The Stakes Couldn't Be Higher,'" *Hollywood Reporter*, February 26, 2020, https://
www.hollywoodreporter.com/features/inside-disneys-bold-200m-gamble
-mulan-stakes-couldnt-be-higher-1280999.

39. Rebecca Davis, "China's 'Mulan' Fans Welcome News of Release Delay," *Variety*, March 13, 2020, https://variety.com/2020/film/news/china-mulan-delay
-coronavirus-liu-yifei-gong-li-1203534355/.

40. For details on the success of the *Snow White and the Seven Dwarves* reissues, see Janet Wasko, *Understanding Disney*, 2nd ed. (Medford, MA: Polity Press, 2020), 17–18.

41. Jill Goldsmith, "Disney's Bob Iger Says 'A Few More' Movies Might Be Going Directly to Disney+ After 'Artemis Fowl,'" *Deadline*, April 7, 2020, https://
deadline.com/2020/04/disneys-iger-more-movies-after-artemis-fowl-going-to
-disney-1202902982/.

42. Dade Hayes, "Disney Says More Movie Releases Could Skip Theaters,

Sees 'Some Changes' to Release Strategy during and after COVID-19," *Deadline*, May 5, 2020, https://deadline.com/2020/05/disney-says-more-movie-releases -could-skip-theaters-vows-some-changes-to-release-strategy-amid-covid-19 -crisis-1202926837/.

43. In 2019 North America was the largest theatrical market, but effective October 2020 it was surpassed by China. See Patrick Brzeski, "China, the World's Second Largest Film Market, Moves beyond Hollywood," *Hollywood Reporter*, October 7, 2020, https://www.hollywoodreporter.com/news/china-the-worlds -second-largest-film-market-moves-beyond-hollywood.

44. Pamela McClintock, " 'Mulan' Sets Sail on Historic Dual PVOD-Theatrical Journey," *Hollywood Reporter*, September 2, 2020, https://www.hollywoodrepor ter.com/news/mulan-sets-sail-on-historic-dual-pvod-theatrical-journey.

45. For more on theater owner responses, see Tom Grater, "UK Cinema Owners Blindsided by Disney 'Mulan' Decision: 'It's a F*ck You to Exhibitors,' " *Deadline*, August 5, 2020, https://deadline.com/2020/08/uk-cinema-owners -blindsided-disney-mulan-decision-1203004622/; and Tom Grater, "French Cinema Owner Destroys 'Mulan' Pop-up Art in Protest against Disney Decision to Skip Theaters," *Deadline*, August 6, 2020, https://deadline.com/2020/08/french -cinema-owner-destroys-mulan-pop-up-art-protest-disneys-decision-skip-cine mas-1203005960/.

46. Anthony D'Alessandro, " 'Mulan' PVOD Results: Disney CEO Bob Chapek 'Pleased,' but Stays Mum on Numbers," *Deadline*, November 12, 2020, https://dead line.com/2020/11/mulan-pvod-bob-chapek-revenue-viewership-1234613878/.

47. Wayne Friedman, "Disney's 'Mulan' Scores $33.5 Million in Streaming Labor Day Release: Industry Estimate," *Media Post*, September 9, 2020, https:// www.mediapost.com/publications/article/355547/disneys-mulan-scores-335-mil lion-in-streaming.html.

48. For more on the histories of location shooting and Hollywood's use of for-eign settings, see Steinhart, *Runaway Hollywood*.

49. For more on Disney's attempts at diversity and inclusion in its films, see Wasko, *Understanding Disney*.

50. Shawna Kidman, *Comic Books Incorporated: How the Business of Comics Became the Business of Hollywood* (Berkley: University of California Press, 2019), 10–12.

CHAPTER 3. EXHIBITION

1. Caetlin Benson-Allot, *The Stuff of Spectatorship: Material Cultures of Film and Television* (Berkeley: University of California Press, 2021), 133–170.

2. Nancy Tartaglione, "Coronavirus: How Hollywood Is Navigating Un-charted Waters as Cases Spike in Korea and Italy Forcing Release Delays and World Wide Box Office Sees Possible $4B Loss through March," *Deadline*, Febru-ary 26, 2020, https://deadline.com/2020/02/coronavirus-corvid-19-hollywood

-studios-response-financial-impact-delayed-releases-china-korea-italy-global
-international-box-office-1202867768/.

3. For details on global reopening dates, see Ben Dalton, "Cinema Reopening Dates around the World: Latest Updates," *ScreenDaily*, December 3, 2020, https://www.screendaily.com/news/cinema-reopening-dates-around-the-world-latest-updates/5149917.article.

4. Tom Grater, "China Orders Re-Closing of All Theaters Nationwide," *Deadline*, March 27, 2020, https://deadline.com/2020/03/china-orders-re-closing-all-cinemas-nationwide-1202894103/.

5. For more on China's reopening, see Anthony D'Alessandro and Nancy Tartaglione, "How China Is Reopening Movie Theaters Faster during the Pandemic," *Deadline*, July 16, 2020, https://deadline.com/2020/07/china-movie-theaters-reopening-coronavirus-imax-wanda-1202987824/.

6. Rebecca Davis, "China Is World's First Market to Achieve Full Box Office Recovery, Says Analytics Firm," *Variety*, August 27, 2020, https://variety.com/2020/film/news/china-first-box-office-recovery-1234751777/.

7. For more on the ways that Indian media culture is unique within global media culture, see Nitin Govil, *Orienting Hollywood: A Century of Film Culture between Los Angeles and Bombay* (New York: NYU Press, 2015); and Aswin Punathambekar, *From Bombay to Bollywood: The Making of a Global Media Industry* (New York: NYU Press, 2013).

8. For more on the contemporary Indian streaming landscape, see Scott Fitzgerald, "Over-the-Top Video Services in India: Media Imperialism after Globalization," *Media Industries* 6, no. 2 (2019), https://doi.org/10.3998/mij.15031809.0006.206.

9. For more on Netflix in India, see Lobato, *Netflix Nations*.

10. Lang and Rubin, "What Happens If Coronavirus Causes Movie Theaters to Close?"

11. Speculation about bankruptcy was frequent in April; see Todd Spangler and Rebecca Rubin, "AMC Theaters Bankruptcy Likely, Analysts Say," *Variety*, April 9, 2020, https://variety.com/2020/film/box-office/amc-theatres-bankruptcy-likely-1234575780/; and Rebecca Rubin and Brent Lang, "Can AMC Theaters Afford to File for Bankruptcy during the Coronavirus Pandemic?," *Variety*, April 14, 2020, https://variety.com/2020/film/news/amc-theatres-bankruptcy-analysis-coronavirus-1234578940/.

12. Erich Schwartzel, "'Trolls World Tour' Breaks Digital Records and Charts a New Path for Hollywood," *Wall Street Journal*, April 28, 2020, https://www.wsj.com/articles/trolls-world-tour-breaks-digital-records-and-charts-a-new-path-for-hollywood-11588066202.

13. Anthony D'Alessandro, "Theater Owners Accuse Universal of 'Destructive Tendency' and Not Involving Circuits in 'Trolls World Tour' PVOD Decision," April 28, 2020, https://deadline.com/2020/04/trolls-world-tour-theater-owners-slam-universal-over-pvod-release-1202920128/.

14. Adam Aron, "Letter to Donna Langley—April 28, 2020," reprinted in Pamela McClintock, "AMC Theaters Refuses to Play Universal Films in Wake of 'Trolls: World Tour,'" *Hollywood Reporter*, April 28, 2020, https://www.holly woodreporter.com/news/amc-theatres-refuses-play-universal-films-wake-trolls -world-tour-1292327.

15. Rebecca Rubin and Brent Lang, "Does Anyone Win in AMC Theaters' Fight with Universal Pictures?," *Variety*, April 29, 2020, https://variety.com/2020 /film/news/amc-theatres-universal-pictures-dispute-movie-theaters-1234592899/.

16. Brent Lang, "Cinemark Isn't Sold on AMC-Universal Early VOD Deal," *Variety*, August 4, 2020, https://variety.com/2020/film/news/cinemark-amc-uni versal-vod-early-1234724808/.

17. Rebecca Rubin, "'This Is a Real Kick in the Shorts': Small-Town Theater Owners React to AMC's VOD Pact with Universal," *Variety*, July 31, 2020, https:// variety.com/2020/film/news/universal-amc-theaters-vod-deal-independent -cinemas-1234721612/.

18. Rubin, "Small-Town Theater Owners React"; and Kim Masters, "Producer Jason Blum on Hollywood's WarnerMedia Upheaval," *The Business*, December 14, 2020, https://www.kcrw.com/culture/shows/the-business/jason -blum-warnermedia.

19. Mary McNamara, "I Can't Wait to Go Back to the Movies, but AMC's 15-Cent Tickets Could Be Dangerous," *Los Angeles Times*, August 14, 2020, https:// www.latimes.com/entertainment-arts/story/2020-08-14/amc-reopening-15-cent -movies-covid.

20. Brent Lang, "AMC Theaters Boss: 'We've Survived the Corona Crisis,'" *Variety*, August 6, 2020, https://variety.com/2020/film/news/amc-theaters-cor onavirus-crisis-1234728092/.

21. For historical examples of exhibition cultures, see Kathryn Fuller, *At the Picture Show: Small-Town Audiences and the Creation of Movie Fan Culture* (Charlottesville: University of Virginia Press, 1996); and Lauren Rabinovitz, *For the Love of Pleasure: Women, Movies, and Culture in Turn-of-the-Century Chicago* (New Brunswick, NJ: Rutgers University Press, 1998).

22. John Fithian, USC's the Future of Entertainment Series, interviewed by Alessandro Ago, February 19, 2021.

23. For more on this program, see the Cinema Safe website, https://www .cinemasafe.org.

24. AFAI mission statement, Ciné website, https://athenscine.com/afai.

25. Tom Brueggemann, "Finally, Here Are Some Real VOD Box Office Numbers—And They Show Promise," *IndieWire*, May 8, 2020, https://www.indie wire.com/2020/05/vod-numbers-box-office-kino-lorber-bacurau-1202229710/.

26. Brent Lang and Rebecca Rubin, "Christopher Nolan Wants *Tenet* to Revive Movie Theaters: Will It?," *Variety*, May 7, 2020, https://variety.com/2020 /film/news/christopher-nolan-tenet-movie-theaters-reopening-july-coronavirus -1234599723/.

27. T. L. Taylor, *Watch Me Play: Twitch and the Rise of Game Live Streaming* (Princeton, NJ: Princeton University Press, 2018), 6.

28. Todd Spangler, "Watch-Party Startup Scener Now Supports 10 Streaming Platforms, Raises $2.1 Million," *Variety*, October 1, 2020, https://variety.com /2020/digital/news/scener-watch-party-disney-plus-hbo-max-netflix-1234787891/.

29. Anthony D'Alessandro, "U.S. Box Office Walloped Wednesday with 5,000 Theaters Dark, though Drive-Ins Have Some Gas," *Deadline*, March 19, 2020, https://deadline.com/2020/03/coronavirus-box-office-wednesday-drive -ins-movie-theater-shutdown-1202888223/.

30. Dave McNary, "'The Wretched' Passes $1 Million Mark after Strong Drive-In Theater Buzz," *Variety*, June 7, 2020, https://variety.com/2020/film /news/the-wretched-drive-in-movie-theaters-box-office-1234627414/.

31. Kristen Chuba, "Inside the Drive-In Premiere of Dave Franco's Directorial Debut: 'So Much More Fun Than Putting On a Suit,'" *Hollywood Reporter*, June 19, 2020, https://www.hollywoodreporter.com/rambling-reporter /inside-drive-premiere-dave-francos-directorial-debut-1299427.

32. Tom Cruise, August 25, 2020, 3:07 p.m., https://twitter.com/TomCruise /status/1298336338434052096.

33. Manori Ravindran, "'We'll Do Anything to See *Tenet*': Meet the Fans Taking Flights for Christopher Nolan's Latest," *Variety*, August 26, 2020, https:// variety.com/2020/film/global/tenet-christopher-nolan-flights-flying-1234749449/.

34. Georg Szalai, "Analyst Calls 'Tenet' Domestic Box Office 'Positive Indicator of Demand,'" *Hollywood Reporter*, September 14, 2020, https://www.holly woodreporter.com/news/analyst-calls-tenet-box-office-positive-indicator-of -demand-amid-pandemic.

CONCLUSION. WHERE DO WE GO FROM HERE?

1. Miguel Poiares Maduro and Paul Kahn, "Introduction: A New Beginning," in *Democracy in Times of Pandemic*, ed. Miguel Poiares and Paul Kahn (Cambridge: Cambridge University Press, 2020), 3.

2. Peter Labuza, "Four Ways a New Justice Department Repeal May Radically Reshape Moviegoing," *Polygon*, August 7, 2020, https://www.polygon.com /2019/11/20/20974364/justice-department-paramount-decree-disney-netflix -monopoly.

3. For an oral history of #OscarsSoWhite, which amplified some of these discussions about and in Hollywood, see Reggie Ugwu, "The Hashtag That Changed the Oscars: An Oral History," *New York Times*, February 6, 2020, https://www .nytimes.com/2020/02/06/movies/oscarssowhite-history.html.

4. Maggie Hennefeld, "The Work of Art in the Age of Flexible Inclusion Criteria," *Film Quarterly*, September 30, 2020, https://filmquarterly.org/2020/09/30 /the-work-of-art-in-the-age-of-flexible-inclusion-criteria/.

5. Katie Kilkenny, "As Hollywood Scraps Most Internships, Scramble Be-

gins for Few Remote Openings," *Hollywood Reporter,* May 1, 2020, https://
www.hollywoodreporter.com/news/as-hollywood-scraps-internships-scramble
-begins-few-remote-openings-1292722.

6. For accessible reading about pandemics, see David Quammen, *Spillover:
Animal Infections and the Next Human Pandemic* (New York: Norton, 2012); and
Sonia Shah, *Pandemic: Tracking Contagions, from Cholera to Ebola and Beyond*
(New York: Picador, 2017).

INDEX

Page numbers in italic type indicate information contained in images or image captions.